ETHICAL HACKING FOR BEGINNERS

Learn The Fundamentals Of Ethical Hacking &
CyberSecurity

TABLE OF CONTENTS

INTRODUCTION

First of all, I want to congratulate you and thank you for deciding to **invest in yourself and become better.** I want to tell you this guide will take from 0 (in the field of Cyber Security) and lead you to a basic level so that you are aware of the things around us on the Internet every day.

I want this book to change your mentality and how you think and give you a new perspective on things. The concepts explained here are both theoretical and practical. Let me show you a few of the stuff that you are going to learn from this book

- How **Hackers** think
- What are the **five steps** of **Hacking**
- How to **scan devices** in a network
- How to see other people's **traffic** (such as passwords and web sessions)
- How to use **Kali Linux**
- **VPN** and **Cryptography** concepts
- **Website Hacking** and Security
- And many more :)

This book contains six chapters that cover different themes belonging to the basic concepts of Cyber Security. O want you to know that if you are starting for the first time in IT, this book is not the right choice. Why? Because you need Linux (at least average) knowledge, networking, and (slight) programming to understand some of the things I explain here.

That's why I want to tell you (from the very beginning) that: before you learn to break and secure things, it's essential to understand how technology works. Having this in mind, I wish you a lot of strength in what you do. Pull as hard as you can. You will see that you will achieve what you have done with constant work and effort.

As a Gift, I want to give, for FREE, access to my six steps guide on starting (and performing) as an IT Specialist in today's digital world. Claim your FREE guide by accessing this page: **https://bit.ly/IT-GIFT** , or you can scan the QR code:

You can also check out one of my other books on Amazon.com by clicking this link: https://amzn.to/2zE72Wm

I

LET'S TALK ABOUT HACKERS

I suggest that in the first chapter of this book, we start talking about an exciting subject from the Cyber Security world: Hackers. You've heard about Hackers very often online and in the news. Lately, more and more often. Meaning that the number of Hackers (or Cyber Criminals) is increasing, which means that the Security market is growing and the opportunities.

Before discussing in more detail about Hackers, I want to tell you that you'll see me use these terms interchangeably: *Cyber Security*, *Computer Security*, *Information Security,* or **InfoSec**. These are the same thing: **establishing and maintaining the security level** of an IT infrastructure (computer network, server, laptop, etc.)

Okay, but why do we need Security? Because it assures the excellent functioning of an information system for both companies and people (like you and me). In the case of a security incident aimed at extracting

data (information) from a database, the attackers can steal the data and use it in one of the following scenarios (but not limited to them):

1) They can **sell** it on the black market (*Deep Web*)
2) They can use them for **personal purposes** to attack those people to extract their bank information
3) Other personal reasons - *ego, other's appreciation, personal satisfaction* ... yes, many Hackers are doing it for these reasons

Okay, now that we've been talking badly about Hackers or seeing if all the Hackers are evil. Now you may be wondering: "Wait, Ramon, what do you mean by "if...". "Isn't a hacker is not, by definition ... evil? "

Well, I can tell you that... no, it isn't. The term Hacker (first mentioned in the '80s) defined a person in love with technology, especially those who loved computer programming (aka. writing code). The term (at Cracker was that time) used for people who programmed viruses, broke websites, or did illegal stuff was **Cracker**. You don't hear it anymore. Cracker (today) is associated with an individual trying to crack/find passwords (e.g., Wi-Fi, database passwords, etc.).

Before we move on, I want to remind you that the general term used (generally by the media) is **Hacker,** and the process he's doing is known as "**Hacking**."

Hacking is the process an attacker follows to gain **unauthorized access** to a system (e.g., server, network, laptop, etc.)

These are the terms to have in mind from now on. I hope you've made a clearer picture of the CyberSecurity world, and I suggest we dive even deeper into this topic. Let's talk more about Hackers.

How many types of Hackers are out there?

As I said earlier: **NOT** all Hackers are evil. But if they're not all bad, how do we categorize them? Why is this term even used? How do we know if a "Hacker" is good or bad?

Well, there are three main categories of hackers:

- Black Hat Hacker
- Gray Hat Hacker
- White Hat Hacker

And in the next section, we are going to break down each of the three categories of Hackers:

1) Black Hat Hacker

I'm sure you've heard about these types of Hackers before. Maybe not in this "Black Hat" format (Figure 1.1), but you've undoubtedly heard of them. These are the Hackers everyone refers to when it comes to that term. The people you see in the that are said to have hacked the servers of the X, Y, Z company.

Figure 1.1

Figure 1.1 above illustrates the "logo" of a "Black Hat" hacker, a **non-ethical** person. Usually, those just starting with the Cyber Security and Pen Testing (Penetration Testing) world are default in this category because they don't have experience and are eager to **learn** (also, they don't know what they are doing). These guys are also known as *Script Kiddies* (they only use tools and programs created by other highly skilled individuals).

Many of the Black Hat Hackers hack to make themselves feel better. You can say that hacking, for them, is a selfish act. Let's not forget that this is an **unethical way** of doing things, and no one should intend to do it. In this book, I vigorously promote White Hat Hacking (aka. Ethical Hacking) for many reasons (we'll talk about them later in this chapter).

So besides ego, why are Black Hat Hackers... hacking, anyway? The main reason would be money. These guys steal the **data** and **sell** it on the black market ("Deep Web") or use it for personal purposes (theft, spam, etc.).

2) Grey Hat Hacker

Gray Hat hackers (Figure 1.2) are right in the middle: they are not good, but not bad. What does this mean? It means that they **are not 100%** committed to doing bad things and usually are on the good side (aka. Ethical Hacking).

Figure 1.2

These people focus on learning and on improving themselves. Thus, they often do things wholly and illegally non-ethical (on servers, someone else's network without that person/organization's approval). It's not necessarily for the money or to steal the data or any other stuff. It's just for the experience and the problem-solving activities you're involved in. As an Ethical Hacker, you have a lot of barriers and interdiction (like generating reports), and it's not always fun. But as a Black Hacker (in this case, Gray), there are no limitations, and you are free to test (and eventually learn new stuff and improve your skills).

My recommendation would be to create (or rent) your labs. You can buy equipment (like Routers, Switches, and Servers) and install them into your local network or create a virtual lab in programs such as <u>GNS3</u> or <u>EVE-NG</u>. If you don't want to invest your money, I suggest you try both programs and see what works best.

3) White Hat Hacker (aka. Ethical Hacker)

Unlike the other two categories we've been discussing so far, "White Hat Hackers" (illustrated in Figure 1.3) are the **Ethical Hackers** (the good ones). They "break" specific infrastructures and networks (servers, laptops, smartphones, etc.) to discover vulnerabilities that, generate reports, and notify the developers (or administrators) to fix them.

Figure 1.3

At some point, White Hackers were either "Black Hat" or decided to act from the start as "White." The hack (in an ethical way) and fight for a "cleaner" Internet without security incidents. They are also known as "**Penetration Testers**" because that's their job. They penetrate systems (network, servers, etc.) to find vulnerabilities that can be exploited.

They either work in a freelance form or as employees for the company. What I want to say to you is this:

To do penetration tests (generally speaking... Hacking), ethical hackers must have a contract that gives them the right. The agreement must be between them and the company that wants such a test (on their servers or network) with apparent timelines (when testing begins, at what time, in what areas of the company, etc.) so that it does not jeopardize IT infrastructure.

At the end of the penetration testing process, a **report** (with vulnerabilities found) will be created and handed to the responsible person in the organization.

II

THE HACKING PROCESS

Generally, when talking about Hacking, there is a very well-thought-out structure in the back. We do not want to find a server and "jump" directly on it because we have too little information about it and we are at risk of being caught if we do not take into account the five steps in the process.

How does the Hacking process work?

I hope you notice I have said "the Hacking process," which can take a few days, weeks, or even months (depending on the target and the risk). This process, as I said earlier, consists of 5 steps (Figure 2.1):

1. **Reconnaissance** - Information Gathering
2. **Scanning**
3. **Gaining Access**
4. **Maintaining Access**
5. **Covering Tracks**

Figure 2.1

And now, let's take one turn and talk about each one:

1) Reconnaissance - "*Information Gathering*"

One of the essential things that Hackers do when they decide to attack a system (server, network, etc.) is to gather as much data as possible about it.

Think in the following way: when you want to go for a holiday in a place/country where you have not been, what are you doing? Most likely, you do homework. You mean you're interested in that location. You are looking for different things on Google (what you can do there, such as weather/food, reviews of places in the area, etc.). In other words, you **inform yourself about your target.**

Through this process, a hacker passes when he decides to attack a system. There are different ways to learn more about a site/server, one of the simplest methods is to search Google for information.

With a simple command like **nslookup** (or **dig**), you can find out the site's IP address, and with the whois command, you can find out more about that domain.

> **nslookup** google.com

> **whois** google.com

The term Reconnaissance (or Information Gathering) comes from the idea of researching, informing you about a particular topic before moving on to action. In short, it means **documenting** before the **activity**.

As a matter of time, this process is most "expensive". Why? Because an attacker needs to be very well informed, he needs to know things in detail because otherwise (as we said in step # 5) risks his freedom.

2) Scanning (the system)

The next step in the "Hacking Process" is **scanning**. Once a Hacker has more information about his target, he will begin to learn more (technically this time). And how will he do that? Using various tools (such as Nmap) to scan networks & servers, and provide more precise information about network topology, used equipment, operating system, etc.

Why are they important? Why is it essential for a Hacker to know if a particular web server is running on Windows or Linux? Because once it has this information, it can go further (step 3) with a bit of research on Google to discover some existing vulnerabilities and try to take advantage of them to gain access to that system (or to extract specific data).

We'll talk more broadly about scanning and how we can do this in Chapter 6. Using these scanned data, the Hacker will move to step # 3.

3) Gaining Access

The hacker can start the attack by doing the themes (done research, scanned networks/servers, learning information from different sources - Google, Facebook, Forums - about the target). The attack should be very well thought to be in stealth mode (without triggering alarms and - if possible - without generating too many logs).

There are a lot of **tools** (*Burp Suite, SQLmap, Metasploit,* etc.) that can be used to generate a cyberattack. Everything depends on technology and objective.

Getting access can be done in several ways and from several points of view:

- Gaining **root** access to a Linux server
- Obtain access to a **site's** administration **panel**
- Obtaining **access** to particular network equipment (Router, Firewall, Switch, etc.)
- Get **access** to a network's **end device** (smartphone, tablet, laptop, etc.)

Once the hacker has access to one of the items listed earlier, he has infiltrated the network. He can get a lot of information about the organization he is in (digital).

We will discuss in Chapter 5 more about some types of cyber attacks and how we can do them.

4) Maintaining Access

Once in the network, Hacker has the option of retaining access. In many situations when different servers of major companies (Yahoo, Google, Microsoft, etc.) have been broken, Hackers have always left open doors to get back into the system.

These wickets are called "**backdoor**" and are left intentionally by Hackers (or even by the software developers of any applications that you and I use day by day) to have access later in the system.

So they can constantly extract data, track what's happening in organizations, hold back control, and then do something with these data (usually, they are being sold on the black market on the Deep Web).

After this process, step #5 is critical.

5) Covering Tracks

This is a necessary process (the "Trace Coverage" feature). A process that many Hackers (especially those who are at the beginning of the road) omit. They are simply not mindful (or aware) of covering their tracks and getting caught (in the US, by the FBI, CIA, or the NSA) and punished in court for their deeds.

I repeat that **unauthorized access** to a system can lead to serious criminal consequences:

- confiscation of computer goods - laptops, external hard drives, etc.
- placing under supervision
- or even arrest, these being just some of the consequences

In order not to leave such traces with the possibility to be discovered, here comes a key element: *TO UNDERSTAND HOW THE TECHNOLOGY WORKS*

What am I talking about? I refer to the fact that it is extremely important to understand how "that database server, that mail or web server" works - both in terms of how you configure it and monitoring and logging it.

It's also important to know how to run the **Windows** or **Linux** operating system. "How are users created? Where are their data stored? Login data? What happens when you log on to such a system? Where are those logs written? "

Hacking (professional, ethical and safe) is *not for everyone*, and that's why you have to be very well prepared because, in some situations, your freedom can be put into play.

Another very important thing I want you to remember is that no one, **NO ONE**, does "Hacking" from their **home**. It's essential to hide your tracks as much as you can. This is to change your location and use VPN services and/or Tor for encryption and traffic anonymity.

How do we delete tracks in a system?

Now let's look at how you can cover our footprints once we have entered a system (network, server, laptop, etc.)

- Delete logs from different applications (web, mail, etc.)
- Delete User Logs
- Delete logs from different monitoring systems

Each system has different ways to monitor it for debugging or troubleshooting in the event of a problem

To do this, it is not necessary, as a hacker, to go step by step from file to file to look for and delete the latest logs. But it can use different existing scriptures (on the Internet) of other people with whom they can clean up their traces.

Here's (https://vidstromlabs.com/freetools/) an example of a **Windows** program (also, you can use the Event Viewer from any Windows machine) that does the job for you :)

On **Linux,** you can use the following commands:

#**rm ./bash_history** - to delete the commands given by the current user

#**vim /var/log/messages** - a place where you can delete the generated logs

Or in any other file in **/var/log**, it depends on which application was attempting to exploit. Another way to delete the logs is by using Meterpreter (an application for PenTesters).

6) (For the ethical) Reporting

Another essential step, especially in the Ethical Hacking process, is # 6, Reporting, the step in which Hacker generates a report on the vulnerabilities found (and exploited), suggestions for improvements (bug fixing), and other information that will lead to solving and secure the system.

These were the five steps (6 for Ethical Hackers) that **make the Hacking process**. The next chapter will discuss the three fundamental elements underlying cyber security.

III

INSTALLING AND USING THE

HACKER'S OS KALI LINUX

If you're curious to find out how to make cyberattacks, you've come to the correct chapter because now I'm going to show you a tutorial to install Kali Linux (the Linux distribution used by Hackers).

What is Kali Linux?

Kali Linux is the **Linux distribution** (most) used by Hackers and Professional Pen Testers due to the number of pre-installed programs. In Kali Linux, you can find a lot of programs focused on security and the vulnerability testing side. Whether we're talking about scans, DoS attacks, Web attacks, or any other kind of attack, Kali is the perfect choice for whatever it takes to learn security. In Figure 3.1 below, you can see the official logo of this Linux distribution. The name **Kali** comes from the god of war in Hindu mythology.

Figure 3.1

Although it may seem a little challenging to use at first, it does not have to discourage you from persevering and learning new things. Why do I say it's hard to use? Well, it's Linux, and if you have not interacted with Linux so far (from the Terminal), it might seem quite tricky at first.

Second is a large number of Pen Testing programs on Kali. These are difficult to use (especially at the beginning) if you do not know what their purpose is (basically the technology behind that tool) and if you do not know its syntax (but this can be taught - just like the others).

How can we install Kali Linux?

When it comes to installing any distributions of Linux (so Kali), we have two options:

- Dual-Boot installation
  - Linux and Windows will be installed on different partitions
  - The 2 OSs run one at a time
  - Requires the laptop/desktop reboot to choose the desired OS
- Virtual Machine Installation

o Linux comes installed in a Virtual Box and can be used in conjunction with Windows

o It does not require rebooting, and the two OSes can be used at the same time

o CPU & RAM consumption will be higher

I prefer the 2nd method because it is much simpler and faster. In addition, I tell you from your own experience that if you use the first option, you will often fail to enter into Linux and say, "Let another time. Now I do not want to restart. " But with the 2nd version, you do not apologize. To install Kali Linux, we need to go through a few steps. First of all, we need the **VirtualBox** program (or another virtualization program - ex: VMware Workstation) and the image of the <u>Kali Linux OS</u> (<u>https://www.kali.org/get-kali/</u>) as you can see in Figure 3.2.

I recommend that you select the **64-bit version** and download it using Torrent, for it will be much faster.

Figure 3.2

In the following steps, after downloading the Kali Linux OS image and the VirtualBox program, we are going to:

1. Start creating a virtual machine in VirtualBox
2. Start the installation process, as shown in figures 3.3 and 3.4.

Figure 3.3

If you want to test Kali without installing it, you can choose the **Live** option. The only problem is that every time you start the virtual machine, you will delete the settings/work that you have submitted up to that point. If you write a script and are in Live mode, it will be deleted and not be saved!

I recommend using the classic installation process to save all your data on disk.

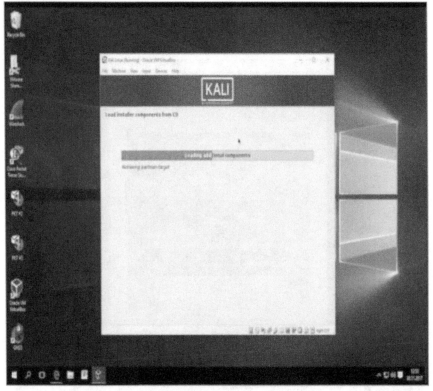

Figure 3.4

Following the installation process (Figure 3.4), you have to go **next -> next -> finish**, and then wait a while until everything is ready. If you do not manage at any time (some settings that you do not understand or are experiencing an error), I encourage you to **research on Google**.

One of the most important skills of our modern times is knowing how to search on Google properly. I'm probably amusing you what I'm saying here, but I want you to know I'm serious about it. From my own experience, this skill has made me very often out of the tangle, regardless of the situation I was in (building the site, finishing the projects during the faculty, documenting and last but not least, finding the forums with topics of interest for me).

So if you get an installation error or any other situation. *Do not panic. Think for yourself. And search on Google :)*

Um .... and by the way, the **default *user*** for Kali Linux is **root** with the **toor** *password*. Now I've missed you a search;)

Working with Kali Linux

Now that you've finished installing and managed to get started and go to Desktop, I propose to move on and briefly introduce Kali so you can understand and identify some of the tools you have at mood (depending on your objective). As you can see in Figure 3.5, we are in Kali's default state, specifically on the Desktop. On the left, you have a bar with some of the tools, but above all (on the 2nd position), you can see the terminal (most probably the most important component that I recommend you to master the best;).

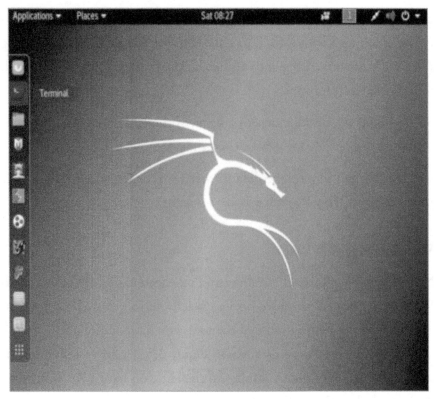

Figure 3.5

Going to the top left, we have a **very interesting menu** :D We can use the Pen Testing application menu (some of you have just experienced the previous chapters). As you can see in Figure 3.6, we have a choice (or even more, they are in different categories, and here we intervene - to choose the most effective programs for our interest).

These applications are "hacking" programs that can be used with good or bad intentions. It all depends on you to use them for the best (aka. Ethical Hacking).

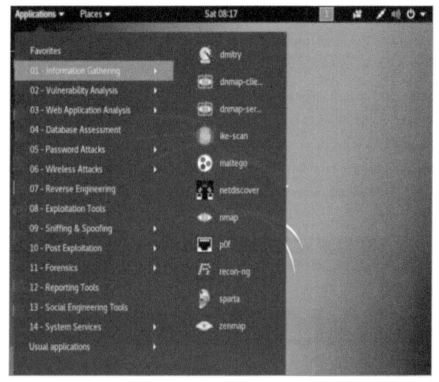

Figure 3.6

And as you can see, the first category is called "Information Gathering", just like the **first step** in the **Hacking Process** (which we discussed in much more detail in Chapter 2). These tools you see in Figure 3.6 help us get more information about our target. Some have even used or mentioned them (nmap, zenmap).

One thing I want you to remember is that when you hit one of these programs (whatever they may be), these two things can happen:

The program opens with the GUI interface

A terminal is running the program opens and displays its "help" information

In the first case, what you can do with it can be intuitive. During use, you will realize it (examples of **GUI programs in Kali**: *Yersinia, Maltego, Burp suite, Wireshark,* etc.).

In the 2nd case, it may not be so obvious from the first use as, as I said before, you will open a terminal with a sort of help/description menu for that tool. In both cases (especially in case 2), it's important to learn that program. Understand what they do and what to eat. In Figure 3.7 below, you can see what I mean:

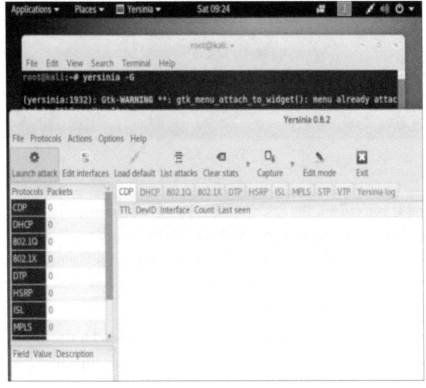

Figure 3.7

Yersinia is a graphical tool with which we can easily make MITM attacks (especially if there are Routers and Unsecured Switches). Yersinia also has a variant in the terminal that is more powerful and customizable. To start the Yersinia GUI version, I have to give the following command:

#yersinia -G

From here, I will let you experiment with this program: D All I can tell you is that on the left side, there will be the number of packets captured by that type (the statistics that give you a clear indication of what type of attack focus).

Going forward, in Figure 3.8 below, you can see another category that contains various tools (some of them used - *ettercap, Wireshark, macchanger*) that aim to listen to or capture traffic in an attack **MITM** (Man-In-The-Middle) type:

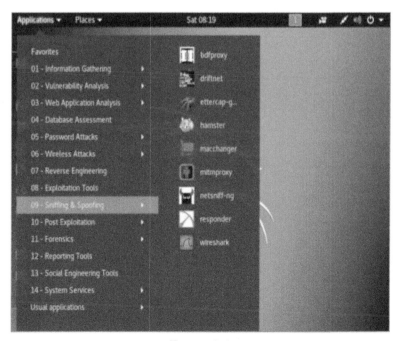

Figure 3.8

This chapter was just a brief introduction to Kali Linux. In the following chapters, we'll take a much more in-depth look at some of these powerful Linux distribution tools.

IV

C.I.A.

Introduction to Cyber Security

In this chapter, we will discuss the three elements that make up the notion of Cyber Security. We will cover her base.

Many people talk about Cyber Security. They just think about encrypting data. It's not necessarily correct because cyber security implies more than that (there are three key elements known as the CIA). This **CIA** is a triad composed of 3 key elements:

- Confidentiality
- Integrity
- Availability

Each of these three elements ensures in one way or another that our data **hasn't been read** (*Confidentiality*), hasn't been **modified** (*Integrity*), and is **accessible** at any time (*Availability*).

1) Confidentiality

When we talk about data **confidentiality,** we will always refer to their encryption to make them **indescribable.** This encryption process requires algorithms with very complex mathematical formulas to ensure that the encrypted data isn't readable.

So if you want to encrypt a file on your phone, laptop or encrypt an Internet communication between 2 networks, things can be done in 2 ways (depending on the situation):

1. **Symmetric** - using a single key (PSK - aka password)
2. **Asymmetric** - using a pair of keys (one public and the other private)

a) Symmetric Encryption

Symmetric encryption is the **most widely used form** of Internet encryption while being fast and secure.

It is so widespread because it requires a single key (called **PSK** - Pre-Shared Key) that will be used for data encryption and decryption. Think of this key as the entrance to your home (you can unlock the door, but you can lock it too).

And now, here is a common case where you use such a PSK to encrypt data (or traffic). This is your wireless connection. Yes, when you first connect to a wireless network (WLAN), it will ask for a password (which is the PSK). That **key** (password) is used for **authentication** and **encryption** of messages.

Now that you understand symmetric encryption, I propose to move on and see some algorithms that make it possible to secure data using a single key:

- DES
- 3DES
- AES
- Blowfish
- RC4

b) Asymmetric Encryption

When it comes to asymmetric encryption, things are a bit different. The **complexity** of this encryption is much more than the symmetric (1024, 2048, or even 4096 bits vs. 128, 192, 256), but the consumption of hardware resources is much higher. Besides, asymmetric encryption uses two **keys** - one **public** and one **private**.

The private key is meant to be ... private, and the public key can be distributed to anyone. Asymmetric encryption is done as follows:

Anything encrypted with the **PUBLIC** key can only decrypt the **PRIVATE** key (so we get data confidentiality).

Anything encrypted with the **PRIVATE** key can only decrypt the **PUBLIC** key (so we get a digital signature to authenticate).

2) Integrity

So, basically, what does data integrity mean?

The integrity of the data ensures that a file can be transferred from point A to point B without altering (or modifying) its content. It is obtained following a process called hashing.

Suppose we have a PDF file that we want to ensure integrity through the Internet transfer. To do this, we need the HASH of this PDF file.

Hash a file helps determine its integrity. When we want to send a file over the Internet, changes can take place along the way (packet loss, alteration of information, hacker changes to content).

Here are some algorithms for determining the integrity of data:

- MD5 - 128 bits
- SHA1 - 160 bits
- SHA2 - 256 bits
- SHA3 - 384 bits (the current standard)
- SHA5 - 512 bits

3) Availability

What value would our data be encrypted and hash if they cannot be accessed? How can we use data if the servers, the network (or the stream: D) are down?

The answer is simple: we could not use them. Then an attack to interrupt data availability can be considered a threat to a company/organization? Of course.

To combat such data security incidents, we have several options that we can implement:

- **Redundancy** - network, server, UPS, etc.
- **Backup**

These two elements underlie the availability of data. Now let's take the first element:

a) Redundancy

There are several types of redundancy, but first, see what Redundancy is like?

Redundancy ensures that for any critical component that assures the company's operation (network, server, power supply, etc.), we have at least one active replacement.

This means that if we have a single router connected to the Internet, to ensure redundancy (at best), we will need two connections to 2 different Internet providers and 2 Routers that connect to these providers.

When it comes to Server-level redundancy, we can think of two or more servers that offer the same services (e.g., web, databases, etc.). Or we can even refer to storage discs (HDDs or SSDs) that can be "linked" together to provide redundancy using a technology called **RAID** (Redundant Array of Independent Disks).

b) Backup

We all know how important backups are - both hard disks (SSD) and site-level, configuration files, code, etc. **Recurring backups** can "save our skin" very often because it copies everything we have lived in a system.

For example, in the case of a Ransomware attack (which), if we do not want to pay the amount required by hackers, the only option we have is the backup (specifically, the restoration of an existing one that will bring that system back to life.

Unfortunately, in this case, if backups *are not done quite often* (at least weekly if not daily), then a partial loss of the most recent changes will be achieved.

We have discussed the basics of data security (both those running through the Internet and those that "stay" stored on a hard disk / SSD).

As a summary of those discussed, I would like to remind you that:

1. **CIA** (Confidentiality - Encryption - Integrity, Availability) is the basis of Cyber Security
2. There are two ways to make **Data Encryption** (Symmetric and Asymmetric)
3. Data **integrity** is established by a **Hash** (which is a unique value for any sequence of information)
4. It is extremely important to ensure the **Availability** of data. A few ways we can do it is by using Backup and Redundancy elements

V

MALWARE AND CYBER ATTACKS

In this chapter, we start talking about **malware types**, and later on, we will discuss **Cyber Attacks**. For starters, we will discuss Viruses, Trojans, Worms, Ransomware and other types of programs that were badly designed. But first of all, let us answer the following question:

1) What is Malware?

A **malware** (aka. malicious software) is a malicious program designed to steal, destroy, or corrupt data stored on our devices.

Figure 5.1

Many people use the **generic term of the virus**, which is not necessarily correct because there can be many types of dangerous programs.

Here below (only) a part of them:

1) Virus
2) Trojans
3) Worms
4) Ransomware
5) Spyware
6) Adware
7) and many more (Rootkit, time bombs, backdoor, etc.)

Here is the picture below on *Wikipedia*, the proportion (in 2011) of malware from the Internet. Since then, many things have changed, but it's interesting to have such a hierarchy with the most common types of malware.

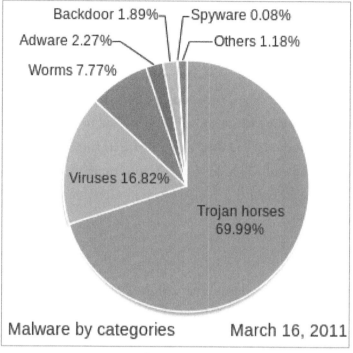

Figure 5.2

And now take some of this malware and discuss them in more detail:

1) Viruses

A virus is a program to which we are all accustomed. Whether we had the computer infected with a virus or we heard/seen someone else, we know that these viruses can be really dangerous (especially for our data stored on the computer - the most important element for us).

Virus programmers take advantage of existing vulnerabilities in different operating systems (especially Windows) and write software to take advantage of them (and users of these devices).

2) Trojans

A Trojan is a program designed to appear for the benefit of the person who uses it, but there is a malicious code behind it that has other intentions altogether. These programs are most common on the Internet (as you can see in the picture above) and are used to being easily masked in front of an inexperienced user. So in the (first) run of the program, the trojan is installed and will hide, doing its job "quietly". The term Trojan comes from the story of the Trojan horse in Greek mythology, exposed in the movie Troy.

3) Worms

A worm is a form of malware that will do its best to expand and infect others on the network once it infects a device (PC, laptop, server, etc.). Thus, a worm manages to **slow networks, connected devices** (CPU and RAM resources), and even the network because infected computers will generate abnormal traffic.

4) Ransomware

Recently, ransomware is a more popular type of malware whose purpose is to **encrypt victim's hard disk** (or SSD) and request a cash **redemption** for the decryption key.

5) Adware

Once installed on a device (or in the browser), some programs will start to show commercials (annoying).

6) Spyware

Spyware is a program designed to extract specific information from users. They are not meant to hurt (by consuming resources) or affect the victim in any way but simply extract data and send them to "mother servers" (those who have initiated "espionage").

First, you need to be aware of such programs, after which you have to take protection/prevention measures against them.

In this situation, anti-virus programs are very welcome because they have very large databases (known as virus signatures) that check every program/file on your computer.

Now you know that Windows has the highest number of malware (viruses, Trojans, ransomware, etc.). Why? Because Windows is the most widely used operating system globally, globally something to "steal." That's why the main focus of attackers and cyber-security companies is on Windows.

Mac and Linux are also not free from malware, but their number is not that big. They have been designed with a higher degree of security and completely differently from Windows.

2) Examples of CyberAttacks

This section of Chapter 5 will discuss Cyber Attacks and see some examples of **CyberAttacks** (and hacking methods) on the Internet. These hacking methods are very common, and each one serves a particular purpose.

What is a Cyber Attack?

A cyber-attack is a means by which a person (with bad intentions) takes advantage of the **vulnerabilities** existing on a particular system (server, computer, network equipment, application, etc.)

Here are some of the most common attacks on the Internet:

1) **MITM**-Man in the Middle
2) **DoS**-Denial of Service
3) **DDoS**-Distributed Denial of Service, check this link:
   http://www.digitalattackmap.com/
4) **SQLi**-SQL injection
5) **XSS**-Cross-Site Scripting

In addition, there are many more in the Internet world, but to illustrate some, we will only focus on the top 3. So let's take the first type of attack, MITM, and discuss it in more detail (and show you some ways you can make such attacks - but please do it ethically). After that, we'll go further with the discussion of DoS and DDoS.

After all, in Chapter 6, we will discuss web security and other types of attacks: SQL injections and XSS.

What is a MITM (Man In The Middle) attack?

MITM is a type of cyber-attack that allows the hacker to eavesdrop on the network traffic of one or multiple devices from the same LAN (Local Area Network).

What does this mean? If you go to a café bar in town and connect to the same Wi-Fi as other people, you can intercept their network traffic from a couple of Linux commands (e.g., login passwords to platforms such as Facebook, Google, etc.).

That's how it is, but do not worry because things are not that simple. Why? Because the vast majority of our Internet connections are secured (**HTTPS instead of HTTP**;)), instead it does not mean that there can be no one listening to your traffic.

To avoid such situations, I recommend using a VPN in public places. In Figure 5.3, you can see an example of a MITM attack:

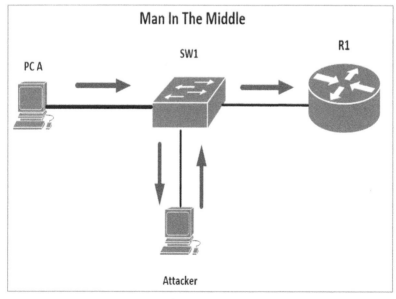

Figure 5.3

There are several ways you can do MITM (I will list below just a few of the many possibilities below):

- MAC Spoofing
- ARP Spoofing
- Rogue DHCP Server
- STP Attack
- DNS Poisoning

These are some of the most common. In the following, I will discuss some of these and give you a couple of examples of how to do it.

1) MAC Spoofing

The term spoofing comes from deceiving, and it refers to the deception of at least one device in the network by pretending to be another computer (or even the Router) by using its MAC address.

It can be done easily by using an app that changes your MAC address with a PC to see its traffic. Here's an example (https://windowsreport.com/mac-address-changer-windows-10/) on Windows 10 about how to change your MAC address, but in my opinion, the process is much more complex compared to Linux:

```
# ifconfig eth0 down
# macchanger -m 00:d0:70:00:20:69 eth0
# ifconfig eth0 up
```

First, we stop the interface (eth0 in this example), then use the **macchanger** command that helps us with the **MAC address change**, and the -m argument lets us specify an address. For verification, use the command: **#ifconfig**

PS: If you want to generate a random MAC, then use: #macchanger -r eth0

2) ARP Spoofing

ARP Spoofing works similarly to MAC spoofing, just as the attacker uses the ARP protocol to mislead the entire network about having the MAC address X (which is the Router). Thus, all network devices that want to reach the Internet will send the traffic to the attacker (redirecting it to the Router). In this situation, the attacker can see all the traffic passing through him using a traffic capture program such as Wireshark.

In Figure 5.4 below, you can see how this process takes place:

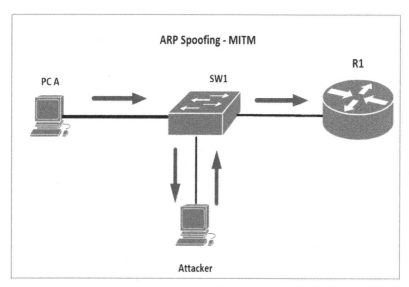

Figure 5.4

To initiate such an attack, first, we must **start the routing process on Linux** to send the traffic from the victim to the Router and vice versa (through us, the "attackers"):

```
# echo "1" > proc/sys/net/ipv4/ip_forward
# cat /proc/sys/net/ipv4/ip_forward
```

Now we are **redirecting** the traffic to the port we want to listen to:

```
# iptables -t nat -A PREROUTING -p tcp --destination-port 80 -j
REDIRECT --to-port 8181
```

After which we need to install the program:

```
# sudo apt-get update
# sudo apt-get install dsniff
```

And now, we can give the command to start the attack:

```
# sudo arpspoof -i eth0 -t 192.168.1.3 192.168.1.1
# sudo arpspoof -i eth0 -t 192.168.1.1 192.168.1.3
```

- *-i eth0*: is the interface on which we will start the attack
- *-t 192.168.1.3*: is the IP of the victim (the device we want to attack - CHANGE with an IP from your network)
- *192.168.1.1*: is the Router IP (CHANGE the Router IP to your Router)

Virtually these two orders send fake packages to the two devices, informing them that traffic has to pass through the attacker. Now all you have to do is open Wireshark and see how the victim's traffic "passes through you".

Here is another need for an element that will facilitate the **DECRYPTION of traffic**. Why? Because much of the Internet traffic is encrypted.

With this tool, we will use: **SSLstrip** (removes the security element, SSL), and the command to decrypt HTTPS traffic in HTTP is:

sudo python sslstrip.py -l 8181

This command will listen to traffic on port 8181 and try to decrypt it. After that, you can start Wireshark and see the encrypted traffic (however, I suggest you start Wireshark and when the traffic is encrypted to see the difference).

PS: At a simple search on Google, you will find SSLstrip;)

To write the result to a file (from the terminal), you can use a tool similar to Wireshark called **Ettercap**. Once you install it on Linux, you can give the following command:

sudo ettercap –i eth0 –T –w /root/scan.txt –M arp /192.168.1.3 /

The arguments used in the command are:

- *-i eth0*: the interface on which we are going to listen for traffic
- -T : to launch command execution over the terminal
- -M : Man in middle mode
- -w : writing data to a file
- 192.168.1.3: the victim's IP address

3) Rogue DHCP Server

This type of attack involves creating an unauthorized DHCP Server in the network that offers the valid IP address but offers the gateway's IP address, the attacker's address. Thus, each network device (which has requested an IP address dynamically) will send the traffic to the attacker, which will then redirect to the Router. Meanwhile, all traffic can be **decrypted** (by using SSL Strip) and seen using **Wireshark.**

This attack can be made by using (on Windows) a program that allows you to create the DHCP server, and on Linux, you can use the **dhcpd server.** Besides all this, you also need to add a static default route to **redirect** all traffic to the Network Router (aka Gateway).

Here are the steps:

1. Start the Routing process on Kali
   a. # echo "1" > /proc/sys/net/ipv4/ip_forward
2. Install the DHCP server
   a. # sudo apt-get install isc-dhcp-server
3. Configure the DHCP server
   a. # nano /etc/dhcp/dhcpd.conf
4. Add a (default) static route to your Router
   a. # sudo ip route add default via 192.168.1.1
5. Start SSL Strip
6. Capture the traffic

How can we protect ourselves from a MITM attack?

Yes, there is a solution for all these attacks. Several solutions, but I will tell you a relatively simple one that you can use today. It's called VPN (Virtual Private Network) and it will encrypt your traffic without anyone (in the middle) being able to decrypt it.

Another solution applies to Network switches, namely DHCP Snooping or DAI (Dynamic ARP Inspection), which are different mechanisms to rely on specific devices in the network. And if someone wants to break this, they will be penalized by excluding them entirely from the network (closing the port directly from the switch).

What is a DoS (Denial of Service) attack?

DoS is a form of cyber-attack to interrupt (for an amount of time) the operation of a particular service on a server with only **one source of traffic** (the attack will happen on a single computer). The DoS takes place by **sending** an **impressive** amount of **traffic** to a targeted service to interrupt it. Thus, receiving a lot of requests, a web server, for example, would not handle and block at the moment => interruption of the service (in this case, dropping the website). Here's an example of an attack in Figure 5.5:

Figure 5.5

What is a DDoS (Distributed Denial of Service) attack?

DDoS is a form of cyberattack that interrupts (for a while) the operation of a particular service on a server or an entire network with many Internet traffic sources.

DDoS occurs via multiple "infected" computers with malware that send an impressive number of Gbps (10.40, 100+ Gbps - greatly depends on the number of computers) in traffic.

These computers are all over the world and do not have a specific location, which is one of the reasons why DDoS is very hard to fight. Even recently (in February 2018), the biggest DDoS attack in history, cataloging 1.5 Tbps (or 1500 Gbps), has taken place. Wow!

I want you to know that such a network of malware-infected computers is called Botnet. Below is an example of a Botnet that can serve multiple malicious purposes (sending spam or malware or a significant Gbps number for DoS) - Figure 5.6:

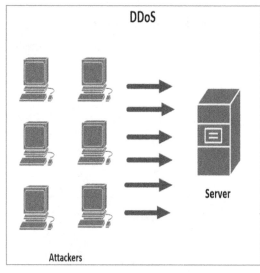

Figure 5.6

In addition to these network-related attacks, there are also attacks to "break" passwords:

1) Brute Force
2) Dictionary Attack
3) Rainbow table

1) Brute Force

Brute Force is a cyberattack that aims to gain unauthorized access to the system (a site administration server, server, network equipment, etc.). This technique uses "brute force," meaning the attacker tries to **guess** the **password** with a minimum of logic behind it. Often, this technique leads to failure and waiver by the attacker, but there are many cases where access to the system has been denied because the admin didn't change the default password (which is often "admin" or "12345678")

2) Dictionary attack

A Dictionary Attack goes a little more targeted on the victim's system because several external factors relate to that organization/person.

With the help of some tools, hundreds or even thousands of words can be generated and used to access the system. The **disadvantage** of this type of attack is that it can take a long time (depending on the number of words and the system's security), and the dictionary does not guarantee the attack's success.

An easy way to **combat** these attacks is to use a maximum number (usually 3) of login attempts in the system.

3) Rainbow table

The third type of attack is called **"Rainbow Table,"** which aims to **"decipher"** a **hash**. Do you still know what a hash is? If not, I'll briefly summarize.

A hash is a unique value of a word (or any combination of letters/digits, etc.). Any combination of letters, numbers, words/phrases in this world will generate a unique value. Now think about your password when entering it into your Facebook, Google, etc., account.

All companies do not store your password directly into their database (because it involves a security risk), but they will store this hash (of the password). When an attacker "steals" the database, he steals it with **username** and *password* **hash** (and not the password in clear text).

Thus the attacker will use a hash list to decipher the hash-passwords from the stolen database. This list is called the "rainbow table" and tries to find out which is the password.

And now you may be wondering, "Why are things so?" The answer is simple: because the hash process is irreversible, that is, once the hash has been generated, we cannot enter it using the same mathematical formula and get the password.

So the attacker tries his luck with his list of hashes (rainbow tables) associated with passwords.

In the next chapter, we'll move on to the first step toward generating a cyber-attack, Scanning. Also, towards the end of the chapter, I will show you how to do a DoS pin attack using (Kali) Linux.

VI

SCANNING THE SERVERS
AND THE NETWORK

I'm sure you've heard of the concept of scanning a network (or the devices within the network). In this chapter, we'll talk in more detail about this subject and later on, we'll see how to **scan networks and servers** (from just a few commands on Kali Linux or a few clicks on Windows).

What does "Scanning a Network" mean?

Before we go over to see how I can scan a network, I want to explain what this scanning means. What do I mean by the end when I say I scanned the X.Y.Z.A network? I refer to the fact that I used a certain program (in this case, Nmap) to find out which devices are connected to the network.

Not only did we find out what these devices are (see their IP address and MAC address), but we can find out more information like:

- The type of the device
- The OS and its version
- Open ports
- Network applications that run on those ports
- etc.

Once we have this information, we can use it to better understand how the network is structured, scan, and then test the network and vulnerability servers (in an ethical way) to make sure all devices are up & running. These, of course, are just a few reasons why scanning the network and the devices in it makes sense.

How do I scan a network?

Scanning the network (and its components) is easy, using Nmap. Nmap comes from Network Mapper and helps us "map" the network into an output (from the terminal) that is quite easy to understand. The program I use in the example below (for scanning the network) is Nmap. **Nmap** (on Windows, the graphical interface program is **Zenmap**) is a free tool extremely used by hackers and ethical hackers.

With its help, we can discover the devices connected to the network, their open ports, and even their Operating System.

Here are some examples of commands that we can give with Nmap to achieve different goals:

1) Scanning a network with Nmap

nmap -sP *192.168.1.0/24* -- ICMP (ping) scanning, displaying the number of network devices (aka **PING SCAN**)

nmap -sS *192.168.1.0/24* -- scanning the entire network to find ports open (TCP, using SYN) on each device (aka **PORT SCAN**)

In Figure 6.1 below, you can see the information about part of the equipment connected to the network (more precisely, the Router with IP 192.168.1.1 and another device with IP 192.168.1.3). Besides discovering that these devices are connected to the network, Nmap has also discovered open ports.

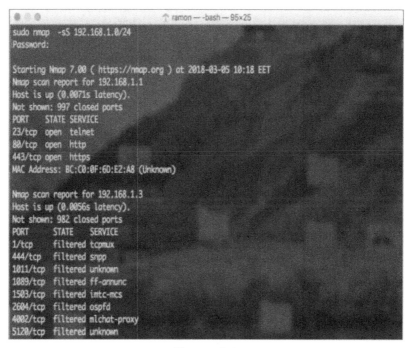

Figure 6.1

As you can see, Router (192.168.1.1) has opened three important services that can be vulnerable and exploited. For example, port 23 represents Telnet, which means we can connect remotely to it and even access the CLI.

Also, ports 80 and 443 that identify Web traffic are open (so we can connect through the browser and try to get access to this Router). Now I hope you understand the role and power of scanning;)

2) Scanning devices in a network with Nmap (server, laptop, smartphone, etc.)

nmap -A *192.168.1.1* -- scans a single device for service delivery (ports) and operating system (aka **OS SCAN**)

nmap -sT 192.168.1.254 -- scans by using TCP packets

nmap -sU 192.168.1.1 -- scans by using UDP packets

In Figure 6.2, you can see the result of the first command we also added and **-sS** for TCP port scanning:

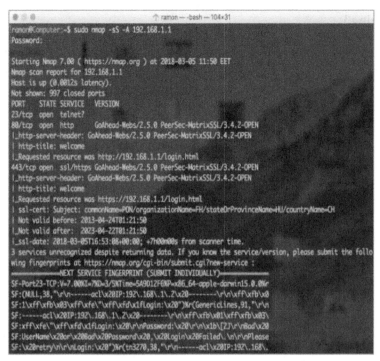

Figure 6.2

If you want to get (more) real-time scan-related information, I recommend you add **-v** to any kind of Nmap command you want.

You can also press "*Space*" to get data on scan progress (you will see X% completed and estimated time). Other examples of scanning using Nmap:

nmap -F 192.168.1.0/24 -- scans every device in the network for the top 100 more used ports

nmap -sS -p 80,443,23,22,25 192.168.1.1 -- scans the device for the ports given with -p using TCP SYN packets

nmap -F -oN *rezultat_scanare.txt* 192.168.1.0/24 -- scans the network and stores the result in the results.txt file (very useful for a Python script)

3) Hping3

Another very useful tool we can use next to Nmap is hping3. **Hping3** is a traffic generator, similar to ping, but with much more functionality. It can send (besides ICMP - ping traffic) packets of the TCP, UDP, or RAW - IP type customized packages (with any specification we tell them about these protocols).

For example, we can send a TCP ACK packet or FIN to see how the server or firewall we want to test reacts. Below is a list of things you can do with this tool.

Practically, hping3 helps us do the following:

- Firewall testing
- Advanced port scanning
- Network testing, using different protocols, TOS, fragmentation
- Manual path MTU discovery
- Advanced traceroute, under all the supported protocols
- Remote OS fingerprinting
- Remote uptime guessing
- TCP/IP stacks auditing

Here are a few examples of **using hping3**:

hping3 -h -- to learn more about the available arguments

hping3 -1 *VICTIM_IP* -- a normal ping (ICMP) is sent (Figure 6.3)

hping3 --traceroute -V -1 *VICTIM_IP* -- a single traceroute packet is going to be sent to see the route toward the destination

hping3 -V -S -p 80 *VICTIM_IP*   -- TCP SYN packets are sent on port 80 to see if the application response

In Figure 6.3 below, we can do some tests and you can see some of the examples outlined above:

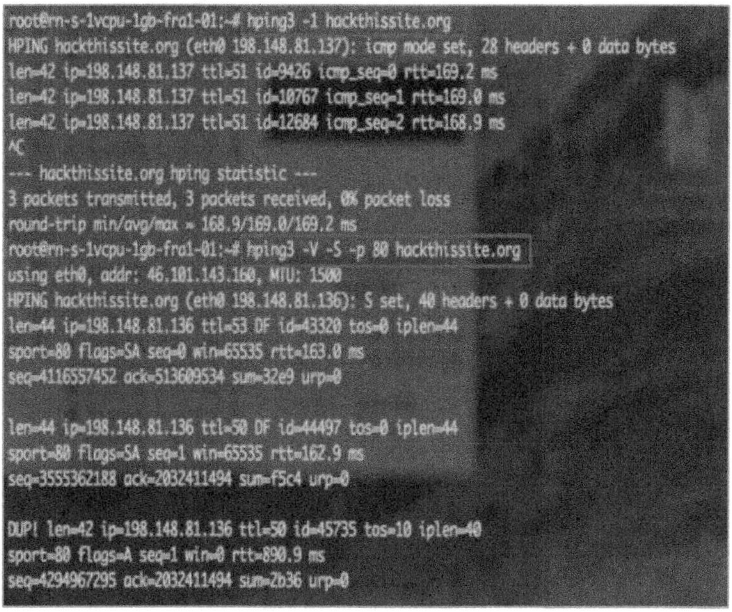

Figure 6.3

hping3 -c 1 -V -p 80 -s 5050 -A *VICTIM_IP*

-- this type of scan sends a single TCP packet of type ACK (-A) and helps us figure out if a device is up on the network when it does not respond to ping (blocked by a firewall).

The arguments of the command (Figure 6.4) represent:

- **-c 1**: sends only one packet
- **-V**: verbose
- **-p 80**: sets the destination port to 80 (HTTP)
- **-s 5050**: sets the source port to 5050
- **-A**: sends TCP ACK packets

```
root@rn-s-1vcpu-1gb-fra1-01:~# hping3 -c 10 -V -p 80 -s 5050 -A hackthisite.com
using eth0, addr: 46.101.143.160, MTU: 1500
HPING hackthisite.com (eth0 52.86.22.136): A set, 40 headers + 0 data bytes
len=42 ip=52.86.22.136 ttl=236 DF id=49647 tos=0 iplen=40
sport=80 flags=R seq=0 win=0 rtt=106.6 ms
seq=1866469472 ack=0 sum=5313 urp=0

len=42 ip=52.86.22.136 ttl=239 DF id=49717 tos=0 iplen=40
sport=80 flags=R seq=1 win=0 rtt=105.5 ms
seq=1569963852 ack=0 sum=1276 urp=0

len=42 ip=52.86.22.136 ttl=239 DF id=49943 tos=0 iplen=40
sport=80 flags=R seq=2 win=0 rtt=105.4 ms
seq=166285298 ack=0 sum=1639 urp=0

^C
--- hackthisite.com hping statistic ---
3 packets transmitted, 3 packets received, 0% packet loss
round-trip min/avg/max = 105.4/105.8/106.6 ms
root@rn-s-1vcpu-1gb-fra1-01:~#
```

Figure 6.4

If we want to **cover our traces** (to be anonymous, not to know where the scanning/attack comes from), we can add the **--rand-source** argument:

hping3 -c 1 -V -p 80 -s 5050 -A --rand-source *VICTIM_IP*

Hping3 allows you to be very specific with what you do. For example, if we use TCP-like scans at the server level, we can use TCP messages (such as SYN, ACK, FIN, RST, URG, etc.).

I repeat what I said at the beginning of this book: *IT IS CRUCIAL TO UNDERSTAND HOW THE TECHNOLOGY WORKS*. In this case, I refer specifically to the OSI model, the TCP protocol, the ports, etc.

But with **packages sent customized** (an unexpected TCP ACK, for example), we can capture the firewall or the application (e.g., the webserver) and give us a response with which we can find more information about it (a server on Windows responds in - a different way than one on Linux, etc. - example of remote OS fingerprinting).

Next, I suggest you play with these Nmap and hping3 programs to do a little more research so you can understand their usefulness and how they work.

With **hping3,** we can also make **DoS** attacks (which we talked about in chapter 5), in which we are flooding a particular device:

hping3 -V -c 2000000 -d 100 -S -w 64 -p 443 -s 591 --flood --rand-source *VICTIM_IP*

And the arguments of this command are:

- --flood: sends the packets as fast as possible
- --rand-source: generates a random source IP address for each packet
- -V: offers more information
- -c --count: the total number of packets
- -d --data: the size of the packets
- -S --syn: TCP SYN packets
- -w --win: window size (default 64)
- -p --destport: destination port
- -s --baseport: source port (by default, it's a random one)

These were just a few examples. You can start playing with this tool (I recommend using Kali Linux and starting with your local network). Instead of IP_VICTIM, you can give your Router IP or a phone/laptop/server from your network.

PS: if you use Linux (and not Kali Linux), you can install Nmap or hping3 using the command:

sudo apt-get install nmap hping3

Why do we want to scan the network?

Because we can use this information to decide our focus on penetration testing, what do we focus on? What is the most vulnerable target in the network and what apps are on it that we can take advantage of? For a hacker (whether ethical or not), the answer to these questions is extremely important.

Why? Because if he is not well informed about the network and its components, Hacker will lose time with certain parts that cannot be exploited and risk being detected.

This scanning process is part of the Penetration Testing cycle, consisting of 5 steps (Figure 6.5).

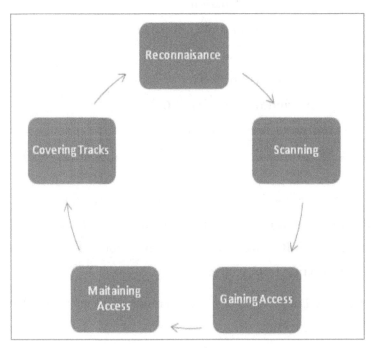

Figure 6.5

VII

WEB SECURITY

In this chapter, we will briefly talk about web security and some attacks that you need to have in mind. I'm sure you've heard a lot of times on TV, radio, or in different parts of the company's X site was broken, the organization's Y site was down and hackers replaced the main site with a page the false one that had a particular message.

Well, I want to tell you that at large (Less Experienced Hackers), they all look for many vulnerabilities known to their sites 1 to 2 that they can take advantage of. Many tools help them locate these vulnerabilities relatively quickly and then help them exploit them.

Some of these vulnerabilities (web-level) are exceptionally well presented and documented in the Open Web Application Security Project (**OWASP**). OWASP is a nonprofit organization dedicated to improving the security of software and web applications.

In previous years, they have a **top 10** with the most commonly reported security incidents on websites and web applications. OWASP organizes even local events (you can research on Google or Facebook for such events), creating a community of passionate cyber security people.

If you hear of such an event and you have the opportunity to go, I recommend you take this step because you will see that it is worthwhile first and secondly that you learn many things from many people.

For example, in Figure 7.1, a list of the most common web security incidents that occurred in 2017 (compared to 2013):

OWASP Top 10 – 2013 (Previous)	OWASP Top 10 – 2017 (New)
A1 – Injection	A1 – Injection
A2 – Broken Authentication and Session Management	A2 – Broken Authentication and Session Management
A3 – Cross-Site Scripting (XSS)	A3 – Cross-Site Scripting (XSS)
A4 – Insecure Direct Object References - Merged with A7	A4 – Broken Access Control (Original category in 2003/2004)
A5 – Security Misconfiguration	A5 – Security Misconfiguration
A6 – Sensitive Data Exposure	A6 – Sensitive Data Exposure
A7 – Missing Function Level Access Control - Merged with A4	A7 – Insufficient Attack Protection (NEW)
A8 – Cross-Site Request Forgery (CSRF)	A8 – Cross-Site Request Forgery (CSRF)
A9 – Using Components with Known Vulnerabilities	A9 – Using Components with Known Vulnerabilities
A10 – Unvalidated Redirects and Forwards - Dropped	A10 – Underprotected APIs (NEW)

Figure 7.1

As you can see, for the most part, it's about the same type of vulnerabilities, with the top changing very little over three years. We will only take some of these attacks and explain what each person represents and how you can do them on your site.

Here are the attacks we will discuss further:

- SQL injection
- XSS
- Security Misconfiguration

Now let's start talking about web attacks with the first attack/vulnerability (and most common) from the list above:

1) SQL Injection

When we talk about SQL injection, we are talking primarily about databases and, secondly, about the attack (a vulnerability) at their level. Let's first look at what SQL is. **SQL (Structured Query Language)** is a query language with databases. It is used to communicate directly with the database through various commands. There are several types/forms of SQL, but the basics are the same.

Practically SQL injection (Figure 7.2) is a way for a hacker to access a database in an unauthorized manner and extract critical information (data about people, username & password, contact data such as emails or bank information, etc.). This situation, in general, is due to a programming error.

Figure 7.2

Where are the SQL injection attacks? These often occur when the attacker finds a "box" in which he can enter data. For example, think about a search box where anyone can write anything.

If the back code (most often PHP) is not written correctly, then the hacker can enter SQL commands that interact directly with the database, so they can extract different information.

Now I want you to think that when you interact with an "input form" (a box where you can write and send something to the server), this happens:

SELECT * FROM ? WHERE ? LIKE '%';

PHP language will generate such an order to interact (and search) with the database. Where '%' appears, it will be replaced with what you enter in that input form.

Here's an example of a SQL code that can be entered in this field (ATTENTION: it will not work for any site. I suggest using the bWAPP application and testing it):

' OR 1=1;--

You can try on **this site** (https://sqlzoo.net/hack/) to enter the SQL statement above instead of the username and password.

SQLmap is a great tool to **test database vulnerabilities** on a site. SQLmap will do all these queries that automatically automate SQL injection for you (and even try to break the hash of the passwords you will find in the database).

I also recommend that you download and install bWAPP (http://www.itsecgames.com/), a web application that contains over 100 classical vulnerabilities (including the OWASP top 10). You can practice this virtual machine (you will connect to it through the browser -> put the IP address of the virtual machine in your browser) without any problems later (you know what I was talking about in chapter 1 ... about hackers?). If you want to install bWAPP on Kali (or any other Linux or Windows distribution), I recommend following these tutorials (https://www.youtube.com/watch?v=XDCZ8FC856s).

2) XSS (Cross-Site Scripting)

When it comes to SQL injection, as you have seen, the attacker goes directly to the site and tries to gain access to his database to retrieve confidential data (usernames and passwords, bank information, mail addresses, etc.). In the XSS case, things happen differently. The attacker focuses on the user (the one who accesses the site) when he uses a script to attack him.

XSS supposes malware injection (malicious script this time) into the site (without affecting it). When accessing the site by the user, this code will be executed directly in the browser. The code is based on JavaScript and can be executed by any browser.

The easiest way to do this is by injecting the malicious code into a comment or script that can be run automatically.

For example, the hacker can intentionally incorporate a link to a malicious JavaScript script in a blog comment.

XSS attacks (Cross-site scripting) can significantly damage the site's reputation by placing users' information at risk without leaving traces of how bad it was. Any sensitive information a user sends to the site (such as personal data, bank information, or other private data) - can be misplaced through scripts on sites without site owners realizing that there is a problem.

Some of the attacks that may occur following an XSS attack:

- **Stealing cookies** - duplication of a cookie may result in duplication of the session from the valid site to a fake site of the attacker that can steal user data
- **Keylogger** - sending all the letters typed by the user to the attacker
- **Phishing** - manipulating the user to take action that is unconscious and then viewing his or her data

So after an attacker tries an XSS attack (usually on any site that has a comment, search, or data input section, etc.), the victim's data (e.g., current web session, cookies) can be stolen and used by the hacker to access different pages/resources. Thus, the attacker does not need his user the victim's password because it already has cookies. Using XSS, he managed to make another type of attack known as **Session Hijacking**.

NOTES: Here's a great site (https://www.hacksplaining.com/) where you can learn more about web attacks. The site was designed to educate web developers to be aware of existing vulnerabilities and show them how to solve them.

3) Security Misconfiguration

Another common problem, and unfortunately, a large part of the world omits it is password-related. YES, in 2022, we still have this problem. Many people do not take security policies that target passwords seriously and (first of all) change default ones and change with a complex password (over eight characters) in alphanumeric characters.

Every extra character that we add to a password increases the complexity dramatically and, at the same time, the difficulty of breaking (or guessing) it.

So my advice, though it seems trivial, is to re-evaluate your username and password on different systems and switch to action to change them. If you can still add another authentication factor next to your password, that would be great.

For example, you can use biometric authentication (fingerprint) or user-based password and token (generally SMS) on your phone, which is much safer than the classic version.

In Chapter 9 (Cryptography), we will discuss more details about the different forms of authentication. Until then, you go into action! In addition, I want you to look at Figure 7.3, where you can see a list of users and default passwords. Here you can find (http://www.routerpasswords.com/) a website with default users and passwords of several network equipment vendors.

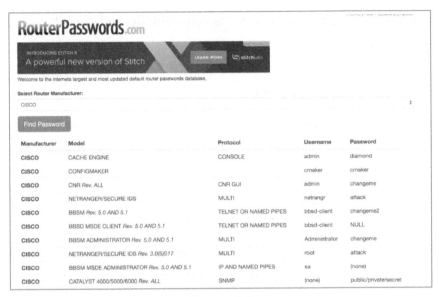

Figure 7.3

Another issue that still appears on many sites is called Directory Listing, which refers to the fact that a hacker can enter your site (more precisely at the back of the site) and can walk from the folder in the folder, so he gets to have access to the site's private information at some point.

This can be a disaster for an online business that sells educational products (books, courses, etc.) so that hackers can access the site and go from folder to folder to search for, download and even delete educational products on the site.

Here comes the security element at the level of folders and files and I mean stopping unauthorized access based on access rights. Each file folder (regardless of Windows, Linux, or Mac) has a set of rules to access it. This way, administrators can allow or restrict access depending on the needs and the level of confidentiality of the file.

Because we are still at the level of website security, I propose to move on and talk about one of the most used platforms for websites. It's about WordPress:

4) WordPress

WordPress (Figure 7.4) is the most widely used website creation and management platform globally. It is a CMS (Content Management System), a content management platform. Thus, anyone can create a blog, a multifunctional online store, or a store. Over 27.5% of the top 10 million sites use it worldwide. Being so widely used worldwide, you realize it is in the interest of Hackers (mainly because this platform contains many bugs and vulnerabilities, which have recently been downgraded from version to version).

Figure 7.4

Another reason why WordPress is so used is the number of existing plugins that can be used to improve the site, user experience, etc. So the person who manages a site/blog using such a CMS does NOT need programming skills because the plugins deal (mostly) with everything needed. There are over 50,000 free plugins available in the WordPress marketplace, and besides these, the paid ones have been developed by different companies.

Another fascinating aspect related to WordPress is that it is Open Source. This means it is developed by a community of programmers in whom anyone can take part.

As for running technologies, WordPress needs **LAMP** (*Linux, Apache, MySQL, PHP*). Each of these components is critical in running a site. If you are not familiar with LAMP, I will briefly explain what each component is:

- **Linux** - The OS on which the site will work, the reason being simple: a flexible, stable OS and more secure than Windows
- **Apache** - The web server used to host the site, most widespread on the Internet
- **MySQL** - The database used by WordPress to store the information site (articles, users, comments and any other type of content that requires storage)
- **PHP** - The programming language that interacts with each component (base data, webserver and OS). PHP is a web programming language used on the backhand side (what we do not see when we access a site)

If you want to install WordPress for your use, you will need a web hosting server. I recommend you use this one (Bluehost) - http://bit.ly/2HvO3je - which provides you with a 1-click install to start immediately using your WordPress site.

After installing WordPress, I suggest we move on to a security scanning tool for your website.

WPScan

WPScan is a scan tool (and, of course, a crack) of a WordPress-based site. It is open-source, so it can be used by anyone who wants to test their site for vulnerabilities. This tool can give you a lot of information about your site:

- The WordPress version used (a good indicator)
- Plugins installed
- Potential vulnerabilities existing on the site can then be exploited
- Finding existing users on the site
- Making Brute Force attacks by using a password finder

Now let's get to work and show you how to do these scans I talked about earlier using **WPScan**. Below are some examples of scanning that you can do with this tool. Attention, while scanning an IP or an URL, *you're not attacking the site.*

Often, scanning can be perceived as actively testing your system to see what you can find through it. You can compare this concept to where someone (stranger) wants to "see" what you have in the house. Enter the door (without you being home) and start looking through your things, but do not take anything to use that information later.

Makes a non-intrusive scan (Figure 7.5):

wpscan --url www.example.com

Enumerates (lists) the installed plugins:

wpscan --url www.example.com --enumerate p

Runs all enumeration tools to learn as much information as possible:

wpscan --url www.example.com --enumerate

List the existing users on the site:

wpscan --url www.example.com --enumerate u

These are some ways to use the WPScan tool. In Figure 7.5 below, I placed my first order on a WordPress-based site (whose identity I will not publish) to see what information we can find out about it. I mentioned that I was authorized to do such a scan on this site.

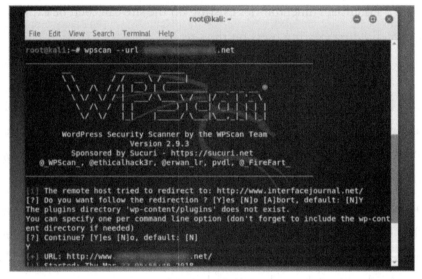

Figure 7.5

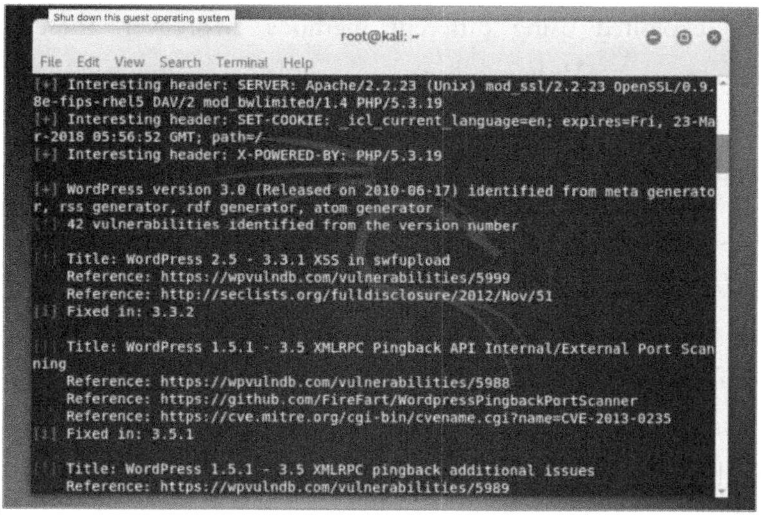

Figure 7.6

Figure 7.7

In figures 7.6 and 7.7, you can see the continuation of the given command. And here, from a simple scan of how many vulnerabilities I found on this site (he needs an update). As you see, many vulnerabilities can be exploited using different methods. Moreover, these **CVE**s (Common Vulnerability and Exposures - https://www.cvedetails.com/browse-by-date.php) also describe the vulnerability and how it can be exploited.

Because we're talking about WordPress and *vulnerabilities,* (https://wpscan.com/) is a database that contains all the **vulnerabilities known** and made **public** for each version. All of the attacks discussed in this chapter also apply to the WordPress case. Unfortunately, *SQLi, XSS, and Traversal Directory* are only a few (of many) attacks that can be done relatively easily on this platform. With WPScan, all you do is find them much faster.

It's important **to be aware** of them, frequently scan your website (yourself or a client), discover new vulnerabilities, and resolve them as quickly as possible.

5) Google Hacking

I think you had a slightly different reaction when you saw the title of this topic: "Wow! can I hack up Google? "or" can I hack with Google? " I can tell you yes, in the 2nd situation (although the first is not excluded). You can use Google to discover different sites that have certain **pages indexed** in the search engine. Thus, using a few specific search keywords, Google can give you exactly what you are looking for (**sites** that contain exactly the **URL** you are looking for with a vulnerable plug-in, a database information page like that be the user, the password and the name of the database, etc.).

Yes, site administrators are not mindful (probably not even aware) of their site being able to **leak valuable information on Google**, exposing it to Internet attacks.

Again, I give you this information because you can use it for ethical purposes (to research and test your site or that of a customer). Do not forget that unauthorized access to a system will be penalized and you may take a few years in prison for this (I know a few people who have suffered this ...).

Now that you have remembered this, here are some examples where you can do research. With this search, Google will display sites with a WordFence plugin (a site security plug-in - firewall, virus scanner, etc.)

inurl:"/wp-content/plugins/wordfence/"

This was just one example (in Figure 7.8). Of course, you can replace search content with "**inurl:**" with whatever you want, depending on your current interest.

Figure 7.8

By following the order in Google Search, you will be able to see different sites depending on the version of WordPress they use. Then you can use WPScan and find out more about the vulnerabilities that exist on it, and then you can try to take advantage of it (ethically). You will see that there are many very old, extremely vulnerable versions of WordPress. I recommend you contact the site admin to make him aware that he is exposed to a massive risk and ask him to let you prove it (that is, attacking his site).

inurl:"wordpress readme.html"

Here, in Figure 7.9, some sites with old versions of WordPress (at the time of writing this book, *April 2018*, the most recent version is **4.9.5**):

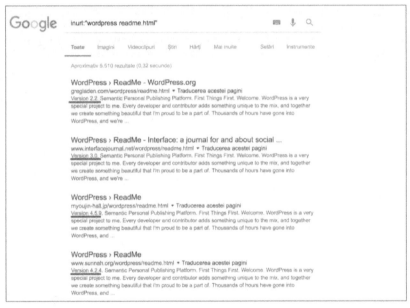

Figure 7.9

I still recommend that you search for yourself. Playing (in an isolated environment or in one that you have access/permission) with all the tools we talked about in this chapter. So, a lot of trouble! :)

VIII

FIREWALL

We start a new interesting chapter about Firewalls and how it works. As long as you work with anything that has to do with servers, networks, and websites, I assure you that you'll meet a lot of Firewalls.

What is a Firewall?

Just like a Router or Switch, a firewall is a network equipment that aims to secure (protect) the network of potential attackers (hackers) from the Internet.

By network security, I specifically refer to packet filtering (source/destination IP address, ports, URL filtering, etc.) to not allow unauthorized access to the network.

By default, a **firewall blocks all external traffic** that wants to get to the internal network (LAN). It is up to the administrator to configure the network access policies required by the company. How does that work? You will find out below;)

One thing you want to know: There is no perfect security, and a Firewall is not enough to secure the network, but it is an important component that helps secure external access (that is, from the Internet to the LAN).

Besides this network element, many other components need to be considered when it comes to security. As shown in Figure 8.1, the firewall connects all the equipment to the Internet (so it takes the Router's place in this situation). Its purpose, in this case, is to protect them from potential attacks from the Internet, which at some point may try to exploit certain vulnerabilities in the systems. The firewall works at level 4 (by default), but it can also be configured to run at level 7 (from the OSI model).

What does this mean? It means you can "look deeper" into the package. Maybe even see what URL you are trying to access and block you, maybe even scan the program you are trying to download and see if it is viruses.

This applies to high-performance and expensive firewalls, **UTM** (**U**nified **T**hreat **M**anagement).

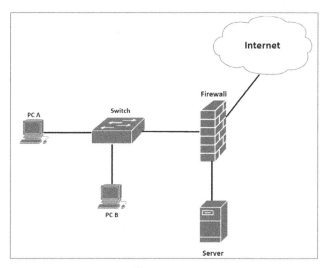

Figure 8.1

How does a Firewall use Security Zones?

The **firewall** divides its interfaces into **security zones**. Virtually every interface of a firewall is a secure area. We can create more such areas and include one or more interfaces. These security zones usually fall into three categories:

- **INSIDE** - the area that includes the internal network (LAN)
- **OUTSIDE** - the area that includes the external network of the organization (usually the Internet)
- **DMZ** - Special Area Containing Servers

The firewall will assign a security level (defined by a number between 0 and 100) to each zone that affects its behavior.

For example, suppose we have an INSIDE area with a security level of 100 and an OUTSIDE area with a security level of 0. In that case, ANY traffic from INSIDE will be left (by the firewall) to go to OUTSIDE (aka Internet). Still, the traffic from OUTSIDE to INSIDE will be stopped, thus requiring special rules (aka. dynamic learning - **stateful** - traffic) that need to be configured on the firewall.

DMZ (Demilitarized Zone) is a special area where the equipment requiring Internet access is placed. Most of the time in this category is the servers (Web, Files, VPN, etc.). These are the company's public resources to which, in theory, anyone has access.

These servers are isolated in a special area (**DMZ**) so that if they get corrupted, the rest of the network will not suffer (the hacker cannot get into the LAN - the company's internal network).

The DMZ has a lower security level (30, as shown in Figure 8.2) than that of the LAN but higher than that of the Internet. So anyone in the DMZ can access the Internet and vice versa because of the firewall rule we will talk about immediately. In Figure 8.2, you can see how these security zones look.

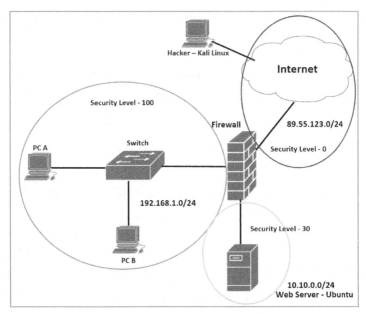

Figure 8.2

Perhaps at some point, you asked yourself, "what does this firewall do 'back'? That is, how does he work? " And I will answer you in the next section about the ACL (basically, this is the "secret ingredient" that protects our new networks), and YES, even your Wireless Router has a built-in mini-firewall that uses ACLs.

ACL (Access Control List)

The ACL is the component underlying the way a firewall works. It is the essential component when it comes to **protecting and filtering traffic** (usually the Internet)

An Access Control List (ACL) is a set of rules to block or allow access from a network to a specific resource. These rules are set to Routers or Firewalls.

"**ACLs** are the fundamentals of security concept (access restriction) in one or a network (e.g., From the Internet to the LAN - or vice versa)."

Think of this concept as a Bodyguard sitting at the entrance of a club where a private party is organized. He will have a list of all the guests at that party.

As people try to get in, the bodyguard will check each one; will look on the list (ACL) and decide for each person whether they are allowed in the club or not. If you are on the list, you will be allowed to come in at the party, and if you do not appear, you will not have access (deny) inside.

To begin with, we need to think about what kind of traffic (aka rules) we want to allow on our network, and then we'll include these rules in the ACL. As we will see below, these rules may vary: from allowing an entire network to access another network to allowing or disallowing a single PC to a server on a particular port (e.g., SSH-22, Web-80).

After such an access list is created and the permissions or deny rules are added, it will be put into operation (such as setting it on a Firewall or Router interface in a certain direction - IN or OUT). IN (side) is firewall traffic, and OUT (side) is the traffic coming out of the Firewall.

Two main types of ACLs can be set (both on Firewalls, Routers and Linux Servers):

- ACL Standard
- ACL Extended

1) ACL Standard

The purpose of standard ACLs is to filter traffic to the IP source! The easiest way to understand is through an example (as in Figure 8.3 and by the way, you can replace these Firewall Routers in your mind, it does not matter, the idea is to understand the concept):

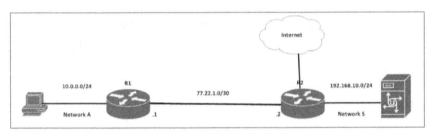

Figure 8.3

Let's say that (for security reasons) the network A PC, with IP 10.0.0.8, and we will not be allowed to access the S-server. So all we have to do is create a list of access to specify this. The rules of this list will look like this:

#**deny** 10.0.0.8

#**permit any**

This rule will be set to R2 on the closest server interface (in this case, the one directly connected to the server) in the OUT direction. We added the 2nd line (allow any) because, by default, at the end of each ACL, a "default deny" rule (#deny any) appears. We want to stop the traffic from the PC to the server and allow any other kind of traffic to rest.

ATTENTION: You do not have to know (or remember) the commands that I'll show you in this section of the book. What's important is that you understand the fundamental of how these ACLs work. Why? Because you will meet them very often. Whether you set them up or whether you want to get through them, it's very important to know how it works.

2) ACL Extended

The purpose of Extended ACLs is to filter traffic by:

1. IP Source
2. IP Destination
3. Port Source
4. Destination Port
5. Protocol (IP, TCP, UDP, etc.)

Thus, this type of list gives us much greater flexibility regarding controlling. We can control any traffic flow regardless of the source, destination, and application used. Here are some practical scenarios

1. In short, ACLs need the following information to put into practice:
2. List along with permit/deny rules according to needs
3. On the interface, we want to apply these rules

4. Traffic direction (IN / OUT) on the interface

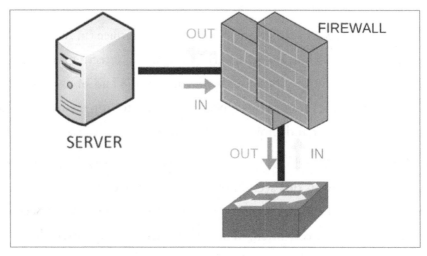

Figure 8.4

As shown in Figure 8.4, the traffic sent from the Switch Network will enter (**IN**) on the Firewall interface and exit (**OUT**) on the interface connected to the Server. The opposite happens when the server responds to the one who contacted it. Now let's resume the image in Figure 8.3

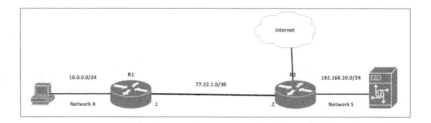

Scenario # 1: Suppose we want to stop the PC (10.0.0.8) from network A from sending any traffic to the Server. In this case, we need a rule that filters after the source IP (ACL Standard). The rules will look like this:

#**deny host** 10.0.0.8

#**permit any**

How do I check the settings? First of all, we will generate ICMP (ping) traffic from PC1 to the server (192.168.10.0), and as we can see in the figure below, it does not work.) Here is proof that R2 blocked traffic. The command # **show ip access-list** indicates that we have eight matches on the deny rule for the PC (Figure 8.5)!

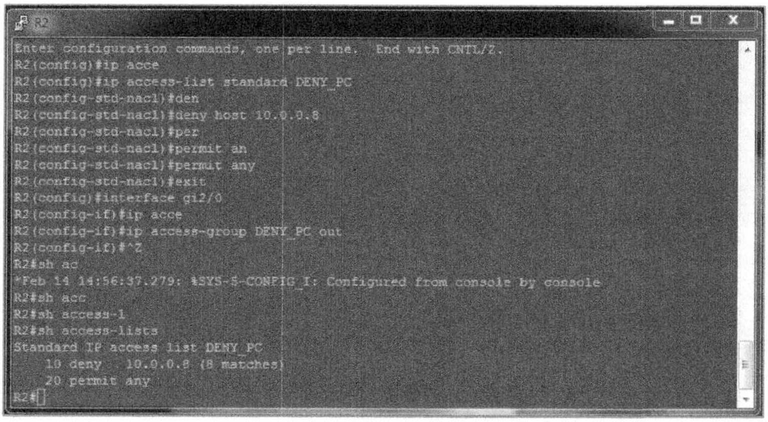

Figure 8.5

Scenario # 2: Suppose we want to stop Web traffic (**HTTP - 80 - and HTTPS - 443**) from the PC network to the Internet. In this case, we need a **more specific rule** (an ACL Extended). The rules will look like this:

#deny tcp host 10.0.0.8 any eq 80

#deny tcp host 10.0.0.8 any eq 443

#permit ip any any

Thus, the first two rules will block Web traffic (ports 80 and 443) for PC to any (any destination), and the latter rule will allow any other traffic from any source to any destination. This rule will be set as close to the source (in the R1 interface connected to the PC) in the IN direction. We will now generate web traffic (from the PC console to the Server - 192.168.10.10):

Just like above, in Figure 8.6, you can see that web traffic has been **blocked** (**6** matches) in the first line of the list:

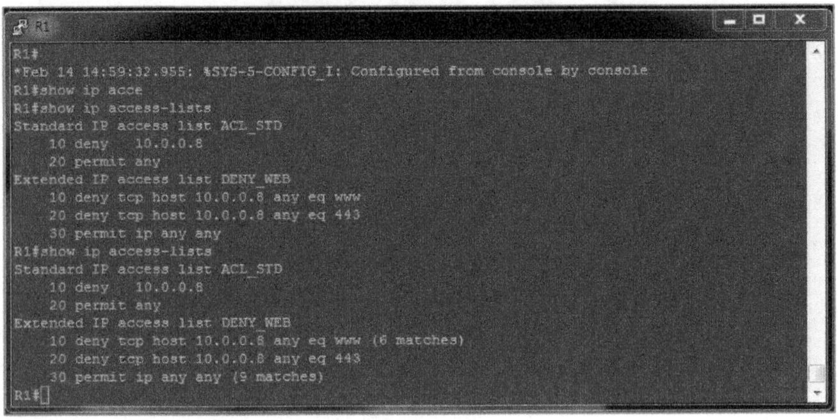

Figure 8.6

Other examples (ACL Standard):

#deny 192.168.99.0/24 -- denies the full range of /24

#permit 85.1.245.5 -- permits only this IP address

#deny 172.16.0.0/17 -- denies the entire network

Other examples (ACL Extended):

#permit ip 172.30.0.0/24 any -- allows traffic from source 172.30.0 / 24 to anything destination

#permit tcp host 10.45.21.5 eq 22 any -- allows any SSH return traffic from 10.45.21.5

#deny udp 172.16.0.0/24 85.98.2.0/23 eq 53 -- blocks DNS traffic (UDP port 53) to the network 172.16.0.0/24 to 85.98.2.0/23

Firewall options available on the market

When it comes to talking about different types of firewalls on the market, we have a wide range of choices (everything depends on our competencies and budget). There are two main categories:

- **Vendor specific** - Cisco ASA, Palo Alto, Checkpoint, Fortinet, etc.
- **Open Source** - pfSense, OPNSense, IP Fire, etc.

Most of these firewalls work similarly (the basic concept is the same). Still, each vendor/developer comes with different elements that make it unique (*artificial intelligence for malware, anti-virus, anti-spam incorporation, URL-level filtering*, etc.). Currently, the market tends to go further towards Palo Alto due to technology innovations on their firewalls and a renowned vendor on the network, remaining behind with its firewall, ASA (Adaptive Security Appliance).

If you want a cheap (even free) solution, good and fast to implement, then one of the variants may even be these **Open Source** firewalls that we will talk about below.

In this section, we will talk much more about Open Source solutions, and as the main example, we will choose **OPNSense** because of the most user-friendly interface.For the beginning, let's talk briefly about pfSense:

pfSense

pfSense is the **most popular open-source firewall** option available on the market. It is used by many companies (even corporations) to protect networks, especially traffic coming from the Internet. At the core of this Firewall is a distribution of Unix, FreeBSD, known in the community to find a highly secure and reliable one. In Figure 8.7 below, you can see what the Firewall configuration interface (**GUI**) looks like.

As you can see, the big advantage is that it has a graphical interface that can be used to make firewall settings. Besides this interface, of course, there is also one in-line command (which can often compensate for the missing graphics - from the browser). In the figure below, you can see the main dashboard of this OS, which at first glance seems a little crowded.

These Open-Source firewalls (pfSense, OPNSense, IP Fire, etc.) can be **installed on your laptop,** on a virtual machine, or even on a two LAN port computer (one used for LAN and the other for WAN - Internet connection). This computer (or older laptop) will be used as a "Router / Firewall" to connect to the Internet and protect your network.

Figure 8.7

Going further, we will discuss OPNSense, an Open Source firewall variant that comes from pfSense (actually a fork - a copy of it - at its initial stage).

OPNSense

OPNSense is another alternative to the Open Source Firewall available on the market (which I prefer more because of the user-friendly interface and design). We will use it to illustrate its functionality in this chapter. From **HERE** (https://opnsense.org/download/), you can download the latest version of this OS, which you can then install on a virtual machine (my recommendation). Select the amd64 (if you have the 64-bit processor), image type: dvd (that's where you will install it locally on a virtual machine), and then you can select what mirror you want (the server from which the file will download installation).

After downloading the OS image, you have two options:

- **Classic installation** (similar to what we did in Kali Linux)
- **Run it Live** - without installing the OS (it WON'T save your settings)

In the beginning, you'll be running Live OS anyway (meaning you will not need to install OPNSense to use it). After you have started the virtual machine with the ISO image of OPNSense, you will get to the interface setting (just as in figure 8.8):

```
You now have the opportunity to configure VLANs.  If you don't require VLANs
for initial connectivity, say no here and use the GUI to configure VLANs later.

Do you want to set up VLANs now? [y/N]:

If you do not know the names of your interfaces, you may choose to use
auto-detection. In that case, disconnect all interfaces now before
hitting 'a' to initiate auto detection.

Enter the WAN interface name or 'a' for auto-detection: em1

Enter the LAN interface name or 'a' for auto-detection
NOTE: this enables full Firewalling/NAT mode.
(or nothing if finished): em0

Enter the Optional 1 interface name or 'a' for auto-detection
(or nothing if finished):

The interfaces will be assigned as follows:

WAN  -> em1
LAN  -> em0

Do you want to proceed? [y/N]: y
```

Figure 8.8

Here, as you can see, we set two interfaces:

- **WAN** - for Internet connection
- **LAN** - for connection to the local network (to the Internet)

This is very important because of the rules set in the background (ACLs and NAT policies are set back to maintain a high level of security and Internet functionality). After setting the two interfaces (which must still exist before starting the virtual machine), ensure that you configure two such Interfaces - preferably in different networks). We are going to log in the Firewall admin console with the **root** user and the **opnsense** password (Figure 8.9):

```
Generating RRD graphs...done.
Configuring system logging...done.
>>> Invoking start script 'newwanip'
Reconfiguring IPv4: OK
>>> Invoking start script 'freebsd'
Configuring additional services: OK
>>> Invoking start script 'carp'
>>> Invoking start script 'cron'
Starting Cron: OK
>>> Invoking start script 'beep'
Root file system: /dev/iso9660/OPNSENSE_INSTALL

*** OPNsense.localdomain: OPNsense 18.1 (amd64/OpenSSL) ***

 LAN (em0)        ->
 WAN (em1)        -> v4/DHCP4: 192.168.1.6/24

Welcome! Both 'root' and 'installer' users are availabe for system
setup or invoking the installer, respectively.  The predefined root
password works for both accounts.  Remote login via SSH is possible.

FreeBSD/amd64 (OPNsense.localdomain) (ttyv0)

login: root
Password:
```

Figure 8.9

Once we have entered the log-in data, we will access the Command Line Interface (CLI) menu of our Firewall that looks similar to Figure 8.10 below:

```
+-------------------------------------------+
|     Hello, this is OPNsense 18.1          |       @@@@@@@@@@@@@@@@
|                                           |       @@@@        @@@@
| Website:     https://opnsense.org/        |       @@@\\\    ///@@@
| Handbook:    https://docs.opnsense.org/   |       )))))))   ((((((((
| Forums:      https://forum.opnsense.org/  |       @@@///    \\\@@@
| Lists:       https://lists.opnsense.org/  |       @@@@        @@@@
| Code:        https://github.com/opnsense  |       @@@@@@@@@@@@@@@@
+-------------------------------------------+

 0) Logout                         7) Ping host
 1) Assign interfaces              8) Shell
 2) Set interface IP address       9) pfTop
 3) Reset the root password       10) Firewall log
 4) Reset to factory defaults     11) Reload all services
 5) Power off system              12) Upgrade from console
 6) Reboot system                 13) Restore a backup

Enter an option: 8
```

Figure 8.10

At this stage, we have several options (testing connectivity, setting interfaces, changing the root user password and most importantly, accessing the shell - aka. command from FreeBSD). So we will enter eight and get access to the command line. As a Unix-based OS, the command line is similar to the Linux command (commands like - cd, ls, mv, find, grep, ps - also appear here - figure 8.11). Of course, others differ, which are distributed-specific.

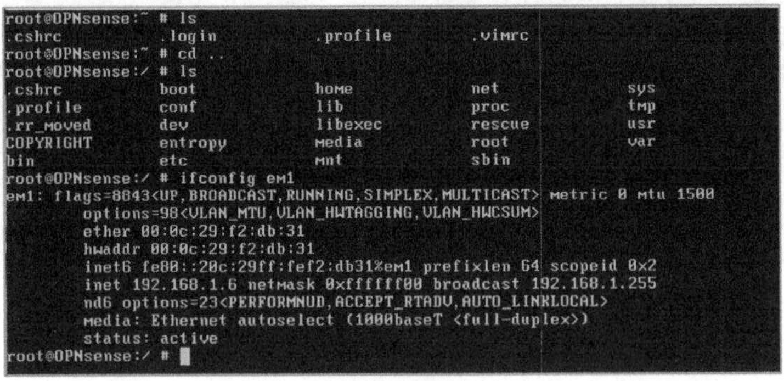

```
root@OPNsense:~ # ls
.cshrc          .login          .profile        .vimrc
root@OPNsense:~ # cd ..
root@OPNsense:/ # ls
.cshrc          boot            home            net             sys
.profile        conf            lib             proc            tmp
.rr_moved       dev             libexec         rescue          usr
COPYRIGHT       entropy         media           root            var
bin             etc             mnt             sbin
root@OPNsense:/ # ifconfig em1
em1: flags=8843<UP,BROADCAST,RUNNING,SIMPLEX,MULTICAST> metric 0 mtu 1500
        options=98<VLAN_MTU,VLAN_HWTAGGING,VLAN_HWCSUM>
        ether 00:0c:29:f2:db:31
        hwaddr 00:0c:29:f2:db:31
        inet6 fe80::20c:29ff:fef2:db31%em1 prefixlen 64 scopeid 0x2
        inet 192.168.1.6 netmask 0xffffff00 broadcast 192.168.1.255
        nd6 options=23<PERFORMNUD,ACCEPT_RTADV,AUTO_LINKLOCAL>
        media: Ethernet autoselect (1000baseT <full-duplex>)
        status: active
root@OPNsense:/ #
```

Figure 8.11

Let's connect to the virtual machine (via SSH) from the terminal:

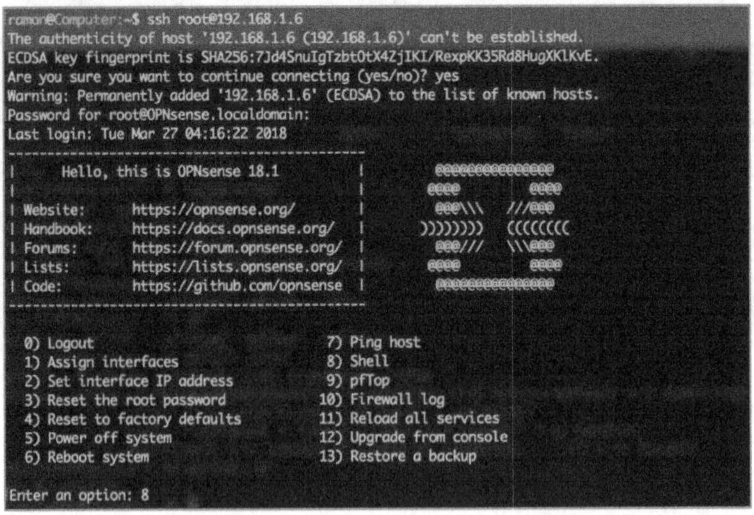

```
raman@Computer:~$ ssh root@192.168.1.6
The authenticity of host '192.168.1.6 (192.168.1.6)' can't be established.
ECDSA key fingerprint is SHA256:7Jd4SnuIgTzbt0tX4ZjIKI/RexpKK35Rd8HugXK1KvE.
Are you sure you want to continue connecting (yes/no)? yes
Warning: Permanently added '192.168.1.6' (ECDSA) to the list of known hosts.
Password for root@OPNsense.localdomain:
Last login: Tue Mar 27 04:16:22 2018
-----------------------------------------
|    Hello, this is OPNsense 18.1         |
|                                         |
| Website:    https://opnsense.org/       |
| Handbook:   https://docs.opnsense.org/  |
| Forums:     https://forum.opnsense.org/ |
| Lists:      https://lists.opnsense.org/ |
| Code:       https://github.com/opnsense |

 0) Logout                   7) Ping host
 1) Assign interfaces        8) Shell
 2) Set interface IP address 9) pfTop
 3) Reset the root password  10) Firewall log
 4) Reset to factory defaults 11) Reload all services
 5) Power off system         12) Upgrade from console
 6) Reboot system            13) Restore a backup

Enter an option: 8
```

Figure 8.12

As you can see in Figure 8.12, we can also connect via SSH, which is turned on by default (if you are on Windows, you can use <u>PuTTY</u> (<u>https://www.putty.org/</u>), and from Linux, you can directly use the terminal and the command:

#**ssh root@**IP_ADDRESS

ATTENTION: By default, OPNSense's **firewall is turned on.** That means it will block your initial SSH traffic. You need to access it from the console (Figure 8.10) and give command #**pfctl -d** (this will stop it).

Now that you have seen some of the OPNSense Firewall (on the command line), I propose to go to the configuration part and adjust its settings through the browser interface. This is how we will add the **IP address of the Firewall** (which we find using the #**ifconfig** command) in the **browser,** after which you will enter your **user** and **password**. See Figure 8.13 below where I am in the main dashboard:

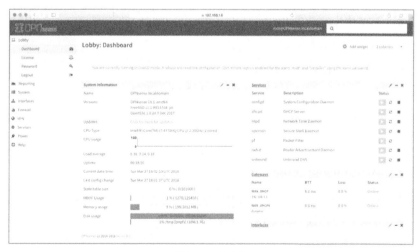

Figure 8.13

Here, at first, there are great chances to redirect you to an installation wizard that will help you set up just a few clicks of the firewall. If you want to configure it so well, you can do it. You can also do it if you want to set up your firewall manually (something you can do after you pass the wizard).

On the left, a list of the menus and sub-menus of each important element on the firewall appears. I want to remind you that this firewall has MANY features and options. My advice is to identify the ones you know and try to configure them (e.g., DHCP Server or settings for LAN and WAN interfaces, etc.).

In the middle of the dashboard, you can see details about the Hardware (CPU, RAM, Disk, etc.) and Software (OS and OPNSense versions), and the **services** that are **currently running** (part of them find the SSH server, DHCP server or Firewall - pf).

Here's a list of some of the things you can do with OPNSense:

- Stateful packet inspection firewall (keeps packets coming out and entering the network)
- IPv4 & IPv6 support
- Security zones (LAN, WAN, DMZ)
- Traffic Shaping
- NAT (Port Forwarding, Static, PAT)
- Redundancy/High Availability
- Load Balancing
- VPN - IPsec, OpenVPN, L2TP
- PPPoE Server
- Real-time graphs for network analysis
- Captive Portal

- DHCP Server and Relay (for IPv4 & IPv6)
- SSH access
- Built in packet capture/sniffer
- Technologies such as VLAN, LAGG/LACP, GRE, PPPoE/PPTP/L2TP/PPP, QinQ

OPNSense even offers internal traffic monitoring tools in the "**Reporting**" area. This was a brief introduction to Firewalls and OPNSense, which is why I let you play with technology.

Next, I recommend building a topology similar to Figure 8.14 and getting started with the various attacks we discussed (e.g., trying to get into the LAN as an Internet attacker). This topology (Figure 8.14) can be done in the **GNS3** (https://gns3.com/) program. Good luck ! ;)

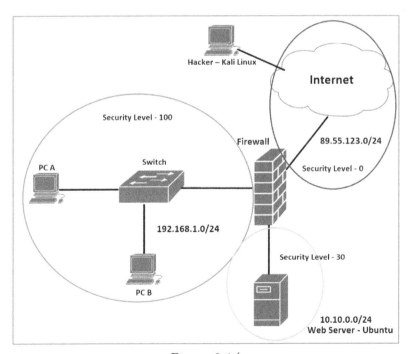

Figure 8.14

IX

INTRODUCTION TO CRYPTOGRAPHY

Cryptography. A trending term (and concept), especially because of the increased interest in Cryptocurrency in recent years. This concept is the basis of everything you do when securing our Internet data. Our data can be in 2 states: moving (traffic through the Internet - sending traffic) and stored (static on an SSD, for example). These data must be secured in one way or another so that they do not reach the hands of an unauthorized person.

Now we will talk about cryptography and resume some of those discussed in Chapter 4 (CIA) (but I will go a little more in detail) because I want things to make sense.

1) Data Confidentiality

When we talk about data **confidentiality,** we will always refer to their **encryption** to make them **unreadable**. This encryption process requires algorithms with very complex mathematical formulas to ensure that they cannot be read. When we talk about algorithms, here are two ways we can do the encryption:

1. **Symmetric** - using a single key (*PSK*)
2. **Asymmetric** - using a pair of keys (one **public** and the other **private**)

a) Symmetric Encryption

Symmetric encryption is the most widely used form of encryption on the Internet because it's fast and secure. It is so widespread because it requires a single key (called **PSK** - Pre-Shared Key) that will be used both for data encryption and decryption.

Think of this key as the entrance to your home (with it, you can **unlock** the door, but you can **lock** it too).

And now, here is a common case where you use such a PSK to encrypt data (or traffic). This is your wireless connection. Yes, when you first connect to a wireless network (**WLAN**), it will ask for a password (which is the PSK).

That key (password) is used for both network authentication and encryption of messages. Now that you understand symmetric encryption, I propose to move on and see some algorithms that make it possible to secure data using a single key:

- DES
- 3DES
- AES

- Blowfish
- RC4

Each of these algorithms uses a key for both encryption and decryption.

DES and **3DES** (**D**ata **E**ncryption **S**tandard) are two encryption algorithms developed in the United States in the early 1970s and have a 56-bit complexity for DES and 168-bits for 3DES. 3DES is not three times safer (or does NOT SECURE 3 times better) than DES, but simply on the same data, apply the DES algorithm three times.

DES and 3DES are algorithms that are no longer used because vulnerabilities have been discovered in them, and the complexity of encryption is much weaker than other algorithms on the market.

In 1999, there was an experiment where decryption ("breaking", "cracking") of a DES-encrypted message was desired, and this was done in less than 24 hours!

AES (**A**dvanced **E**ncryption **S**tandard) is the most popular (and used) symmetric encryption algorithm. It uses a single key (aka PSK) for data encryption and the same key for decryption.

Its key values can be **128, 192, and 256 bits**, all depending on the level of security you want or the ability of the system to make such encryption.

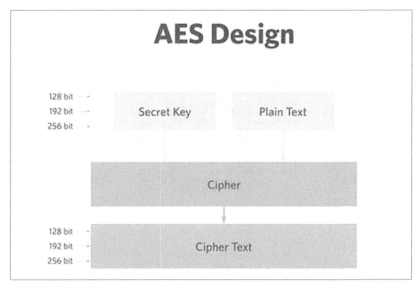

Figure 9.1

In the figure above, you can see how the text/file (which we want to encrypt - Plain Text) is added (together with the secret key) in the AES encryption function (Cipher). The executed text gets the encrypted text (Cipher Text).

b) Asymmetric Encryption

When it comes to asymmetric encryption, things are a little different. The complexity of this encryption is much over the symmetric (*1024, 2048, or even 4096 bits* vs. 128, 192, 256), but the consumption of hardware resources is much higher. Besides, asymmetric encryption uses two keys - one public and one private.

The private key is meant to be ... private, and the **public** key can be distributed to anyone. Asymmetric encryption is done as follows:

Any crypt with the **PUBLIC** key can only decrypt the **PRIVATE** key (so we get data confidentiality).

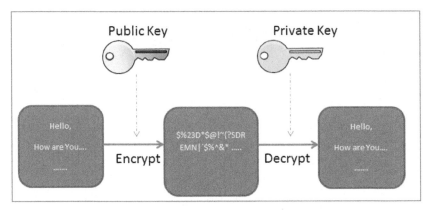

Figure 9.2

And the other way, which does not offer confidentiality or authentication:

Everything encrypted with the **PRIVATE** key can only be decrypted with the **PUBLIC** key. This scenario creates a **digital signature** with the purpose of **authentication**.

Here are some asymmetric encryption algorithms:

- RSA
- DH
- DSA

RSA (**R**ivest **S**hamir **A**dleman) is an **asymmetric** encryption algorithm that uses a key pair: a public one and a private one. This algorithm bears the names of its developers, who developed it in the '70s. Because I was talking earlier about symmetric encryption algorithms (RC4, AES, etc.) where I said they could do 128, 192, and 256-bit encryption keys. Asymmetric algorithms can use much larger keys, their values being 1024, 2048, or even 4096.

The higher the value of the key, the more secure/complex the encryption will be, but it will be slower because it requires more processing power. Otherwise, the encryption principle is the same as described earlier.

DH (Diffie-Helman) is an asymmetric algorithm that aims to generate a symmetric key used to encrypt traffic (for example, this key can be used by 2 Routers that form a VPN tunnel for encrypting traffic between their networks) between 2 entities.

2) Data Integrity

So, basically, what does data integrity mean? The integrity of the data ensures that a file can be transferred from point A to point B without altering (or modifying) its content. It is obtained following a process called hashing.

Suppose we have a PDF file that we want to ensure integrity through the Internet transfer. To do this, we need the HASH of this PDF file.

Follow the tutorial below to learn more about these concepts:

Hash a file helps determine its integrity. When we want to send a file over the Internet, changes can take place along the way (packet loss, alteration of information, hacker changes to content).

So we need a mechanism to ensure that it remains intact (or that the package that arrived at the destination is exactly the one sent from the source).

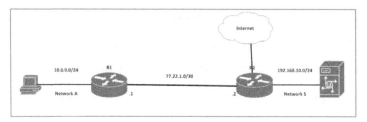

Figure 9.3

Hash helps us accomplish this goal. It is generated by a mathematical formula that obtains a unique ID for any package introduced in this formula.

Thus, when the Source (Server S) wants to send the file to Destination (PC A), it passes through this formula, and the unique ID (aka Hash) is forwarded to the destination (PC).

When this file reaches its destination, Destination recalculates the file ID. If the two values (or IDs) - sent/received - are the same, the package is the same (aka and has retained its integrity).

In the example, we saw how encryption could help us hide the file content, but this is not enough to secure it completely so that anyone can add data (bits) to that file that will alter the content. In this chapter, we were able to see how we protected data from such an attack mechanism by using the hashing technique.

Here are some algorithms for determining the integrity of data:

- MD5 - 128 bits
- SHA1 - 160 bits
- SHA2 - 256 bits
- SHA3 - 368 bits (the current standard)
- SHA5 - 512 bits

Here is the figure below, as shown by a random (random) hash introduced by the mathematical formula of SHA2:

This online tool allows you to generate the SHA256 hash of any string. SHA256 is designed by NSA, it's more reliable than SHA1.
Enter your text below:
So insisted received is occasion advanced honoured. Among ready to which up. Attacks smiling and may out assured moments man nothing outward. Thrown any behind afford either the set depend one temper. Instrument melancholy in acceptance collecting frequently be if. Zealously now pronounce existence add you instantly say offending. Merry their far had widen was. Concerns no in expenses raillery formerly.
Name were we at hope. Remainder household direction zealously the unwilling bed sex. Lose and gay ham sake met that. Stood her place one ten spoke yet. Head case knew ever set why over. Marianne returned of peculiar replying in moderate. Roused get enable garret estate old county. Entreaties you devonshire law dissimilar terminated.
Generate
Clear All
Treat each line as a separate string
SHA256 Hash of your string:
349C7E2068C4CBE950BC72285D2E51EA0D5AB00E248661ACD4BF7E03D64EC3BF

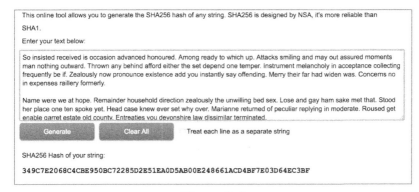

Figure 9.4

And here's another example in which I have the same text, but I deleted one letter (first - S):

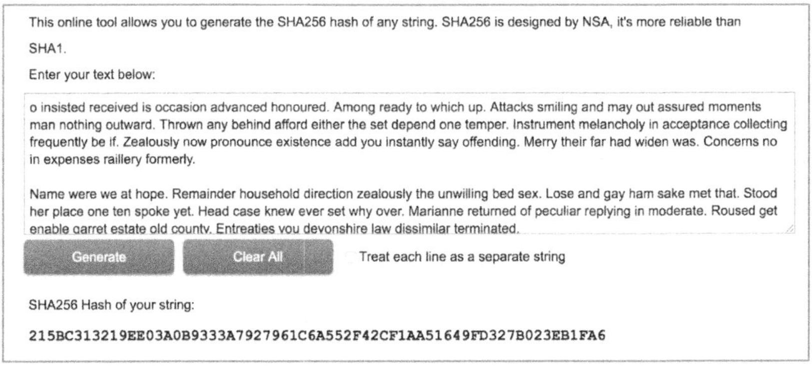

This online tool allows you to generate the SHA256 hash of any string. SHA256 is designed by NSA, it's more reliable than SHA1.
Enter your text below:
o insisted received is occasion advanced honoured. Among ready to which up. Attacks smiling and may out assured moments man nothing outward. Thrown any behind afford either the set depend one temper. Instrument melancholy in acceptance collecting frequently be if. Zealously now pronounce existence add you instantly say offending. Merry their far had widen was. Concerns no in expenses raillery formerly.
Name were we at hope. Remainder household direction zealously the unwilling bed sex. Lose and gay ham sake met that. Stood her place one ten spoke yet. Head case knew ever set why over. Marianne returned of peculiar replying in moderate. Roused get enable garret estate old county. Entreaties you devonshire law dissimilar terminated.
Generate
Clear All
Treat each line as a separate string
SHA256 Hash of your string:
215BC313219EE03A0B9333A7927961C6A552F42CF1AA51649FD327B023EB1FA6

Figure 9.5

As you can see in the two figures, the two values are different. So for any small change (e.g., 1-bit changes), the Hash value will be UNIQUE!

HMAC

HMAC (or **H**ashed-based **M**essage **A**uthentication **C**ode) is a special technique that combines two security elements into one: **authentication** and **hashing**. In order to generate an HMAC from a text, you must use a password (secret key or PSK) to complete the hashing process. Without the secret key (aka password), it is impossible to obtain that unique value (hash), so integrity will not be retained. Below is an example of using an HMAC function:

HMAC_MD5("secret key", "I love computer security and hacking") =
= 8bc851757db4f1f59a96025e30224886

HMAC_SHA1("secret key", "I love computer security and hacking") =
= be23d4136734c7e2a04ec43dc1c24d6c98c07fa2

HMAC_SHA256("secret key", "I love computer security and hacking")
=

=

3200766cf751c62b197b8c9ffe52c00d578e7dc0b0d6fc76076b2488c8a
838d0

As you can see, enter the secret key, then enter the data that you want to be hash-look (in this case, I only put an affirmation that I hope you agree to); We gave three examples because each example uses a more **complex algorithm** (MD5 < SHA1 < SHA256) and generates a stronger hash (which is extremely difficult to break especially because it also contains a secret key to be found by an attacker).

As I said earlier, this HMAC usage is a very good (and much more secure) way of **establishing** the **integrity** (of the data that transits the network - e.g., through a VPN, about which we will talk more in the next chapter).

On **this site** (https://www.freeformatter.com/hmac-generator.html), you can generate your hash using the HMAC technique.

Salt

Another interesting technique that helps us to increase the security (difficulty) of passwords (stored in a database), for example, is the **use of Salt in the hashing process.** A randomly generated text is added when the password is hashing to be stored in the database. So any attacker is much, much harder to "break" these passwords using techniques like dictionaries or rainbow tables that we talked about.

The process follows:

1. **Generate** salt in a random fashion
2. **Combine** the salt with the password
3. **Generating** hash after combination (salt + password)
4. **Storing** the hash in the database

This is the process. I want to mention that Passwords are never stored in clear text format in a database (e.g., **MySQL**). These are always "hash-forgotten" (or encrypted, as some prefer to say).

A different way of securing (hiding) important files

If you thought encryption was the only way to hide a file, there are other ways (less secure and used, but there are :)). One of them is **Steganography** which is the technique of hiding a file inside another file. Assumes that the bits of the "hidden" file are mapped through the **"host file" bits**. When this file is going to be sent by mail, it will be almost impossible to detect by the person who receives the file (especially if it does not use a special tool for that) - or for anyone else.

But how can we **detect** a "hidden" file in another file? The way we can detect such a process is by determining the (hash) integrity of that file and comparing the two values.

<u>Here's a tool</u> (<u>http://steghide.sourceforge.net/</u>) you can use to play Steganography.

3) Authentication

Most of the time, authentication can be done in several ways. Perhaps until now, you were accustomed to user authentication and password (or just password). Lately, biometric authentication (based on fingerprint or even face expression) has become increasingly popular.

Here are some ways to authenticate:

- **User** & **Password** (or just password)
- **Biometrics** (fingerprint, eye, saliva, face, etc.)
- Based on **location** (you can access a resource only if you are in a certain location)
- **Time-based** (you can only access a resource at a certain point in time)
- Based on the **token** (a special tool you just own or even the phone)

In short and a little more scientifically, authentication can be done based on the following factors:

- *what you know* (user password),
- *what you are* (biometric),
- *where you are* (location),
- *what you own* (phone, token)
- *the moment in time*

Now I want to introduce some terms that are being used more often (for example, in banks or on authentication on different platforms - Amazon, Digital Ocean, Google, Facebook, etc.). Here I refer to **2FA (2 Factor Authentication)**. And so, **if we combine two different factors** (of those previously expressed), we get authentication in 2 factors.

An example of one-factor authentication (1FA) is using a User and Password. If we want to have 2FA, we can add biometric authentication or a token (only one of them, NOT both).

The more authentication types we add, the more complexity will be, but the security level simultaneously.

WARNING: if we have to go through 3 different steps each time we are asked for a different password, it does not represent **3FA** but authentication through one factor. Why? In this case, to use what we know, passwords (does not combine it with other modes).

What is a Digital Signature?

The **DSA** (**D**igital **S**ignature **A**lgorithm) algorithm is similar to RSA, but it is used to generate digital signatures. This process (digital signature) occurs by encrypting a message/file (by the source of the message) with the private key and sending it to the destination.

The destination will try to decrypt that message with the public key, and if it manages to do this, the message's source will be confirmed (aka, the message comes from the desired entity in the communication).

What are Digital Certificates?

Another way we can authenticate an entity is by using a Digital Certificate. It's a much safer and more reliable method for authentication. Why? The digital certificate is issued by a superior, trustworthy authority that uniquely identifies only one person/entity.

After all, what is a digital certificate? It is an "identity act" of an entity on the Internet. This digital certificate contains the following information:

- The public key of entity A (we take a fictitious example of the entity as A)
- Entity information
- Certificate Authority - the certification authority that issued the certificate
- Protocols used for encryption (AES, RC4, etc.)
- Date of creation and expiration date of the certificate

Now let's talk about all of this:

a) **The public key** is used by the person (B) who receives the digital certificate for encrypting the message back to the entity (A). At the same time, it is used to decrypt the message included in the certificate (which was encrypted with the private key). So, as I said earlier, the message's source is authenticated (aka Digital Signature).

b) **Information** about entity A - information about the organization,

c) **Certificate Authority** (**CA**)- the certification authority that issued the certificate

A CA can be an organization that everyone trusts. So if many other organizations trust this CA, and the CA has confidence in you, then everyone will trust you. That's how the certificates work, and that's their purpose. Basically, in a math format, the scenario would look like this:

$A = C$
$B = C => A = B$

In Figure 9.6, you can see an example of a digital certificate from Wikipedia:

Figure 9.6

PROTECTING OUR INTERNET TRAFFIC
WITH VPN TECHNOLOGY

I'm sure you've heard of the term VPN. This technology was very common the last time when the number of cyber-attacks was on the rise (Cyber Security is beginning to become more and more important). So the topic we are discussing in this chapter is VPN.

What is a VPN?

A **V**irtual **P**rivate **N**etwork (**VPN**) is a tunnel between two Routers / Firewalls (or even a PC, laptop, or phone to a particular server) that provides secure access between two or more networks. In addition to security, the VPN connects the two networks (as if they were directly connected).

Now you might think, "Hmm ... weird, it was different from what I thought! Isn't the VPN that changes the IP address and secures my connection? " My answer is: "Yes, the VPN also does this, but, as you will see, there are several types of VPNs, each with its purpose." We'll talk about this in more detail.

Until then, here is figure 10.1, the classic example of a VPN tunnel over the Internet linking two networks (and securing traffic) - between two organizations/companies (or networks):

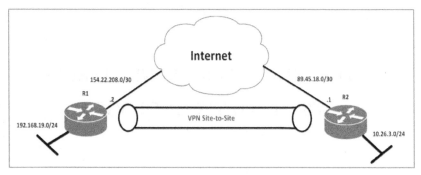

Figure 10.1

With this tunnel, end devices (PCs, laptops, servers, etc.) of the two private networks can communicate securely over the Internet. Virtually the (virtual) connection between the two networks is as if they were directly connected to the same Router.

How does that help us? Simple. If in the 10.26.3.0/24 network (connected to R2 - right) there are several servers (mail, files, etc.), using this VPN tunnel (**created on Routers**), the devices in the 192.168.19.0 network / 24 (left - R1) will have **access** to the **resources** provided by the server.

How many types of VPNs do exist?

In short, two main VPN categories/types exist on the market, namely:

- VPN Site-to-Site
- Remote Access VPN

Now I think it would be a good idea to talk about each one separately: D

1) VPN Site-to-Site

What you saw earlier in Figure 10.1 is a type of Site-to-Site VPN. Why? Because it connects 2 locations (sites - NOT web, but networks) differently as if they were directly connected. A VPN makes you **anonymous** (change the IP address with some "false") and secures the connection of all devices that send traffic from the R1 network to the R2 network and vice versa. This type of VPN uses IPSec (Internet Protocol Security) for encryption, integrity, and authentication, which we'll talk about later.

The example below (Figure 10.2) shows how a site-to-site VPN topology looks logically. This topology takes place between 3 locations (anywhere in the world). You can see how Router R1 (and the network behind 192.168.19.0/24) connects to R2 and R3. This R1 and his network will have access to the internal resources of R3, R2.

If this is a company, these resources can be Active Directory Server, DNS Server, Mail Server, Skype for Business, etc.

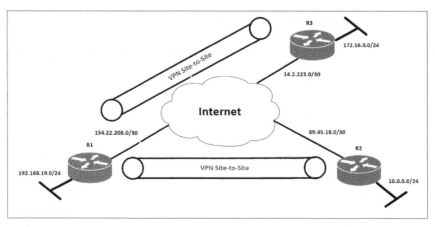

Figure 10.2

2) Remote Access VPN

Now I've come to the type of VPN you probably thought about when you first read the title of this chapter. This type of VPN (as opposed to the site-to-site VPN) is most common because it is handy and relatively easy to configure. There are many VPN providers (such as Bitdefender, CyberGhost, NordVPN, etc.) that offer complete encryption and **anonymity** solution on the Internet. I encourage you to purchase such a service because it will be very beneficial (+ you can use it on your laptop, desktop, or smart device).

Such a VPN is very beneficial if you **care about your security** (especially when you're connected to public Wi-Fi, which, as you've seen in Chapter 5, can be extremely dangerous due to MITM attacks). If you work at a company, it can allow you to work remotely, and if you use your VPN, you will have access to the company's **internal resources.**

As a protocol that secures the connection, SSL (Secure Socket Layer) - or TLS (Transport Layer Security - which also deals with securing our Web, FTP, and so on connections) is the most common reason why SSL is used in this case it is due to the ease of implementation and configuration, compared to IPSec.

In the example below (Figure 10.3), you can see how a Remote Access VPN topology looks (logically). An increasingly common term used for this type of VPN is **Teleworking**. In this example, PC A will have access to the internal resources on R3's network. Unlike the previous example, ONLY PC A has access to these resources.

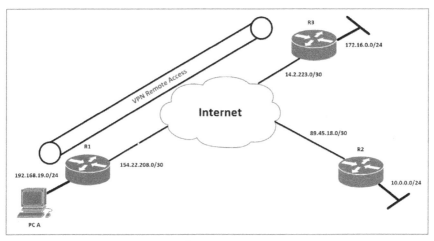

Figure 10.3

When it comes to this type of remote access (VPN), the device you want to connect to a particular network (whether it's a company's internal network or a VPN service bought to protect your identity on the Internet) is necessary to use a program. There are many VPN programs from multiple vendors (*AnyConnect, JunOS Pulse*, even Windows 10 has a built-in VPN client).

You can use many VPN programs (I will recommend two depending on what you want to do). The first program I recommend and you can use on many Operating Systems (Linux, Windows, macOS, Android and iOS) is OpenVPN. It is an **open-source** (and free) solution that uses a configuration file for different connections. The Benefit of OpenVPN is that you can create your VPN connection with a Router (from home, for example) or with your server in a certain part of the world. So you do not depend on anyone. You have full control and it will not cost you anything. Instead, you will need technical knowledge (especially Linux) to set up this type of VPN.

This way of doing VPN can be used either for remote access (to access certain resources) or to secure and anonymous the Internet connection ("stay on the net" with IP from Germany - for example). The choice is yours. I recommend you try both, and it's cool;)

Another VPN solution is the many VPNs that offer different services at different rates. I prefer (and use VPN) **TunnelBear** because it's very easy to use and install, and their application looks cool (+ it offers a free trial solution).

NOTE: This type of VPN gives us **increased security** and **anonymity**. Besides that, we also have access to an Internet area that could be banned (or blocked by firewalls). This type of VPN will keep us from MITM attacks.

Below is a **real example** of using a **TunnelBear VPN** on an iPhone (the same applies to Android, Windows, Linux, or macOS). Enter here (https://www.tunnelbear.com/) to learn more.

As shown in Figure 10.4, I downloaded the app from the App Store (you can also find it on Android). If you want to use this VPN on Windows (or any other OS), you need to create an account here, **download** the **app** and **install** it.

After installing the application, you will be asked to create an account (Figure 10.5) and assign permissions to set up and create this VPN (Figure 10.6). After you pass these steps, it is necessary to check your mail (Figure 10.7), and then you can start using this VPN with a very nice and playful interface (Figure 10.8).

Figure 10.4 & 10.5

Figure 10.6 & 10.7

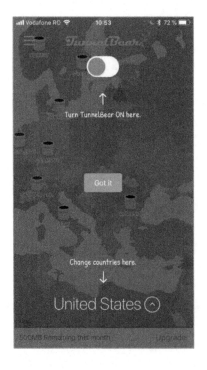

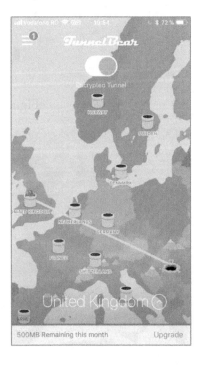

Figure 10.8 & 10.9

Now is the time to choose which country you want to do VPN (this will change your identity and IP over the Internet). As you can see in Figure 10.9, I have chosen the UK, and a very important aspect is the one at the top of the image (between time and Wi-Fi) - that it started the VPN. Figure 10.10 on the next page can confirm this, and I'm looking for Google and displaying UK-related pages.

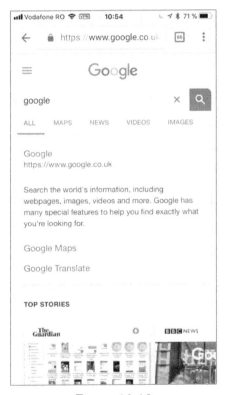

Figure 10.10

This was the process. Simple, right? I encourage you to install TunnelBear on your mobile and laptop/desktop and get familiar with this VPN concept. In the following, we go on with this topic and discuss (more technical) how a VPN works:

How does a VPN work ?

So let's finally see how a VPN works. As I said earlier because a VPN tunnel does its job, it needs security, and this security is achieved through a protocol framework called **IPSec**. These VPN tunnels work on security policy because security is their key. As we will see, these security policies are established with IPSec and generally outline what kind of tunnel tuning is.

What type of encryption algorithm is desirable? What kind of integrity, determination algorithm? How to authenticate (user and password or digital certificates)? Who is going into the tunnel? What are the two devices between which such negotiations should take place?

These are just some of the questions that need a response to form a security policy. And here, there are a lot of possibilities (it depends very much on the level of security you want and the **hardware performance** of your equipment to reach this level).

Security is important and we want more sophisticated algorithms to encrypt (or do anything else) the best, but we forget an important aspect: the hardware performance. Do we have enough strong equipment to make these demands possible? And here, we can refer to **Firewalls, Routers,** or even our end devices.

Also related to VPNs (especially Site-to-Site), there is a concept called **IKE** (Internet Key Exchange). At the time of creating this tunnel (before our traffic is secure), two tunnels are created:

- The first tunnel, to facilitate the safe (secure) creation of the 2nd tunnel
- The 2nd Tunnel to secure the traffic that is to pass through it

IKE helps create these two tunnels (which ultimately form the main VPN tunnel). But it does not do this alone, but with the help of the next security framework.

What is IPSec ?

IPSec (or Internet Protocol Security) is a framework that helps protect (data) information flowing through the Internet. IPSec makes this possible through the four key elements that make up it:

- **Encryption** (Confidentiality)
- **Integrity**
- **Authentication**
- **Anti-replay**

As I said earlier, **IPSec** is a **framework**. Maybe you wonder what this means? A framework is an application structure (IPSec) that accepts add-ons and changes to new protocols.

Whether we are talking about data encryption or integrity, if you and I come up with a new protocol (encrypting or doing one of the procedures mentioned above), then we can integrate it into IPSec to use it to secure our applications (or VPN tunnels).

And now, I'll give you some examples of protocols (included in IPSec) that help encrypt data from a VPN:

- In the case of **encryption,** we have the following protocols:
  - *DES, 3DES*
  - *AES, BlowFish, RC4*
- In the case of **data integrity,** the protocols are:
  - MD5, SHA1
  - SHA2, SHA3
- In the case of **authentication,** we have two main methods
  - User and password
  - Digital certificates

The 4th element (Anti-replay) refers to the fact that the recipient (from an IPSec-based connection) can detect the data fields sent in the first phase. This defense mechanism ensures that the message's source does not retrieve the data for malicious purposes, thus attempting somewhat deny that they were sent in the first instance.

In addition, IPSec is based on two major headers encapsulating the standard IP packet:

- **AH** - Authentication Header (which only establishes integrity and authenticates traffic, does NOT encrypt it)
- **ESP** - Encapsulating Security Payload - Ensures all four elements mentioned above

In Figure 10.11 below, you can see how an AH header looks, its primary role being to authenticate the package. It contains the necessary data for the authentication of each package, IE, and the assurance of its integrity.

IP header	AH header	TCP header	TCP payload / data

Figure 10.11

In Figure 10.12, you can see how the ESP header encapsulates the entire packet and encrypts it (all data from level 3 up to level 7 inclusive).

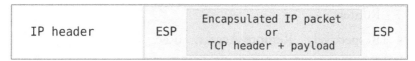

Figure 10.12

Thus, encrypting the entire header, IPSec (in the case of this ESP) adds a new IP field (that is, changing the current IP address with a false IP) to hide the source or destination. Maybe you wonder why this is going to happen? Because the 2 (source and destination) will be anonymous.

When we connect (from your phone or laptop) to a VPN, the connection will be an SSL VPN. Suppose we want to connect two networks between them. In that case, we will form an IPSec VPN tunnel between these 2 Routers. All the equipment in the two networks will be able to communicate with each other (over the Internet - similar to the topology in figure 10.13).

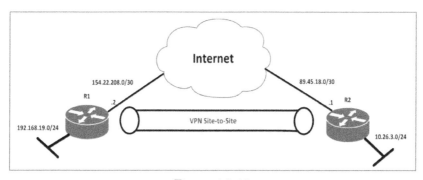

Figure 10.13

I hope you have a much more detailed understanding of what we can refer to as VPN. The fact that there are several types:

- **Site-to-Site** used for network connections for Firewalls or Routers
- Respectively **Remote-Access**, used for end-device remote connections for security/anonymity purposes or to access the internal resources of a network/companies

And a few things about IPSec technology, more precisely, the role of each component of this framework (which I have discussed in more detail in this chapter and the previous chapter):

- Encryption
- Integrity
- Authentication
- Anti-replay

Enjoyed the book? Leave a review!

I would like to thank you for completing this book and reaching the end of it (the majority of people don't get this far). If you received value from this book, I'd like to ask you for a favour. Would you be kind enough to leave a positive review? Thank you!

You can also check out one of my other books on Amazon.com by clicking this link: https://amzn.to/2zE72Wm

Wishing you the best of luck!

Ramon Nastase

IT, Education and Optimism

PS: don't forget to claim your FREE gift here: https://bit.ly/IT-GIFT

Made in the USA
Middletown, DE
19 June 2023

32849457R00076